CW01081593

# The City Where I Want to Live
## Adam Zagajewski

The city is quiet at dusk,
when pale stars waken from their swoon,
and resounds at noon with the voices
of ambitious philosophers and merchants
bearing velvet from the East.
The flames of conversation burn there,
but not pyres.
Old churches, the mossy stones
of ancient prayer, are both its ballast
and its rocket ship.
It is a just city
where foreigners aren't punished,
a city quick to remember
and slow to forget,
tolerating poets, forgiving prophets
for their hopeless lack of humor.
The city was based
on Chopin's preludes,
taking from them only joy and sorrow.
Small hills circle it
in a wide collar; ash trees
grow there, and the slim poplar,
chief justice in the state of trees.
The swift river flowing through the city's heart
murmurs cryptic greetings
day and night
from the springs, the mountains, and the sky.

(Translated from *Without End: New and Selected Poems*, 2002)

**Adam Zagajewski.** Poet, novelist and essayist. Author of *Eternal Enemies: Poems* (2008) and *Unseen Hand: Poems* (2011).

# Europe City

**Lessons from the European Prize for Urban Public Space**

CENTRE DE CULTURA CONTEMPORÀNIA DE BARCELONA

LARS MÜLLER PUBLISHERS

# Lessons from the European Prize for Urban Public Space

## Foreword

## Memory

## Prefaces

## Mobility

## Introduction

## Mixture

"The self-conscious creation of public space as a critical stratagem cannot be sustained over the long term unless it is also combined with public transport."

# On the European Prize for Urban Public Space

## Kenneth Frampton

Unlike the Americas and much of the developing world, Europe has the advantage that much of its historic urban fabric still exists and that despite the universal onslaught of the automobile and the freeway, many towns and villages of the continent still remain virtually intact, including even the centers of late-nineteenth-century metropolises. However, at the same time, we still have to acknowledge that when it comes to the field of urban design it would, in the main, be more appropriate if we were to speak of urban intervention since we no longer have the civic economic power nor, more importantly, the political will, to realize continuous urban form with any degree of consistency. With the exception of enlightened municipalities, here and there, the most we may achieve today is the creation of one-off public places to stand against the universal "non-place" as identified and characterized by Marc Augé in his book *Non-Lieux* of 1992.

However, the creation of sustainable public space has to go beyond the mere provision of a serviceable public amenity, such as a playground or a pocket park. In the last analysis more important are the potential political ramifications of such a space, that which Hannah Arendt so perspicaciously recognized as "the space of public appearance," for public space is not only a physical domain but also a representational form, so that when it is seemingly empty and momentarily unoccupied, it still stands for the community which brought it into being.

All of this could not be further removed from the suburban proliferation of what the American planner Melvin Webber once had the temerity to refer to as the "non-place, urban realm," which, along with his equally apolitical concept of "community without propinquity," was set forth in his influential book *Exploration in Urban Structures* of 1964. One might observe in relation to this advocacy of megapolitan dispersal that the world now consumes in one month the amount of gasoline that it used to consume in the space of a year in the 1950s. With this one realizes that the self-conscious creation of public space as a critical stratagem cannot be sustained over the long term, unless it is also combined with public transport.

Apart from the historic urban core, the universal megapolis presents us with two decidedly opposed paradigms: on the one hand, spontaneous suburbanization which encourages the proliferation of totally unrelated freestanding objects, and on the other, the countervailing model of the megaform, either as a topographic landscape intervention, totally integrated into the given site, or, alternatively, as a public or semipublic building program capable of either enclosing or subtending a public space, as in the now famous L'Illa Diagonal Block in Barcelona realized in 1992 to the designs of the urbanist, the late Manuel de Solà-Morales, in collaboration with the architect Rafael Moneo. Here we have a canonical example of what Solà-Morales used to refer to as "urban acupuncture" in which the megaform brings together the existing economic and topographic potential of the site and the program with some form of ingeniously conceived point ofdeparture or "parti," in which the overall intervention maximizes thetotal potential of the situation. In this regard, L'Illa Block was able to combine a more or less horizontal office building, rising from five to nine floors, with an internal shopping mall extending for eight hundred meters along the main thoroughfare of the Avinguda Diagonal in the center of Barcelona. The net result—serviced by multilevel parking beneath grade—was to create a semipublic marketing facility within its form that was equally accessible to both the historic fabric of the city and the inner suburbs on the periphery. It did all this in such a way as to reenergize the shopping frontage of the avenue itself; to maintain, that is, the promenade of the Avinguda Diagonal as "a space of public appearance."

Nothing is more removed from this catalytic intervention than the large, still unrestricted practice of building single usage shopping centers or malls in the midst of those peripheral suburban developments which surround our historic towns and villages, since the ultimate effect of this supposedly spontaneous, regressive practice is to destroy, in short order, the economic basis of the preexisting civic fabric and with this, of course, the micro-public walkable spaces kept alive by traditional form.

With the alternative stratagem level of an effective landscape or topographic intervention oriented towards the cultivation of the public domain, conceived as a space of public appearance, there is perhaps no more convincing example of recent date than the refurbishing of the space around the Cathedral of Bordeaux in France—the so-called Place Pey-Berland—completed in 2003, to the designs of the Basque architect Francisco Mangado.

Even since the apotheosis of the European provincial city during the first decade of the twentieth century, public transport and above all fixed rail transit has been the occasion for the creation of significant public space. I have in mind in this regard not only Eugenio Montuori's monumental Rome railway terminus, along with the expanse of its plaza set against the antique remains of the Baths of Caracalla, realized between 1947–1960, but also more recently, the new TGV rail heads that emerge today as momentary public realms within the international high-speed rail links throughout the length of the European continent. All of these works and many more not cited in this excursus remain exemplary of what the creation and maintenance of enlightened public space could mean for the future prosperity and political viability of the European Union. One can only hope that the achievements of this Prize to date will encourage other communities within the European continent.

**Kenneth Frampton.** Architect, historian and critic. Ware Professor of Architecture at the Graduate School of Architecture and Planning at Columbia University, New York. Author of *Modern Architecture: A Critical History* (1980, fourth edition, 2007), *Studies in Tectonic Culture* (1995) and *A Genealogy of Modern Architecture* (2015).

# What is the European Prize for Urban Public Space?

The form of the city is closely linked with democracy. This is the basic premise of the European Prize for Urban Public Space, which is a biennial initiative of the Center of Contemporary Culture of Barcelona (CCCB). The Prize acts as a permanent observatory that highlights the civic nature of European public space.

Established in 2000, the Prize is organized in collaboration with The Architecture Foundation (AF), London; Architekturzentrum Wien (AzW), Vienna; Deutsches Architekturmuseum (DAM), Frankfurt; Cité de l'architecture et du patrimoine, Paris; Museum of Architecture and Design (MAO), Ljubljana, and Musem of Finnish Architecture (MFA), Helsinki.

This book is the final project of Europe City, which has been carried out by the CCCB in partnership with the AF, MAO and MFA, with the support of the Culture Programme of the European Union. Europe City has consisted of activities held in Helsinki, Ljubljana, London, and Barcelona that have allowed for an extensive analysis about the results of the Prize and a series of discussions about the democratic values of European cities.

The Prize is organized within the framework of the CCCB's larger, permanent and multidisciplinary program on cities and public space. It has generated numerous publications, exhibitions, conferences and seminars, audiovisuals, and an extensive online archive that records the prolific construction of public space across Europe over the past fifteen years.

**www.publicspace.org**

# Memory and Transformation of the European City

# Vicenç Villatoro

CENTRE DE CULTURA CONTEMPORÀNIA DE BARCELONA

It often happens that when with conviction and enthusiasm we proclaim the virtues and benefits of a certain kind of city, it is because we secretly suspect that this model might be heading for extinction. Or that it is at least threatened. And sometimes, more painfully, we suspect that the virtues of this model might more readily be preserved in the past, when they first emerged, than in a changing present and an unknown future that might become contradictory and thus put them at risk. Hence, for years now, we have been proudly upholding the merits of the European city, successor *inter alia* of the Mediterranean city. This is a compact, continuous, well-balanced, diverse, organic city arising from a process of unhurried sedimentation lasting many centuries, in which the old, historic center has played the dual role of the ancient *agora* as a place of commerce and culture, where things and ideas are exchanged. This interlinking of cities, of many cities—in which they are organized over territories as a structuring network rather than as a hierarchical pyramid—is probably one of Europe's specificities, a mainstay of the continent's culture and one of the bases underlying its economic, political and cultural development. European culture is  the offspring of cities. And every European territory invariably takes the city as its point of reference.

Yet it is precisely when we express this sincere, emphatic praise for the European city that perhaps we begin to realize that our cities are not always as compact or continuous as we claim; not so well-balanced but more sprawling and disperse, with old centers that are sometimes run-down and now devoid of the commercial and cultural activity that once gave them meaning. And we also start wondering whether this denaturing transformation of the old model of the European city is an inevitable change brought about by the citizens' evolving habits in mobility, consumption, leisure, culture, and so on. Now that we have learned that the European city model has such essential virtues, Europe might be starting to betray its own model and, although it is admirable, wondering to what extent it may be sustained.

Over the past fifteen years and jointly with many sound, sensitive European partners, the CCCB has been leading a project to compile positive experiences within the general framework of what the European city model represents. And it has done so through the European Prize for Urban Public Space, which has selected but also kept amassing specific, particularly outstanding projects concerned with cities. Not only the prizewinners, but all the entries presented over a lengthy period—in some editions up to three hundred from more than thirty European countries—have contributed information about how Europe is striving to conserve the positive aspects of its urban model and to bring what needs to be adapted to new realities up to date. Almost without exception, in their various ways the projects considered for the Prize are true to the spirit of the compact, diverse, deep-rooted city that lies at the heart of European memory. But these are also innovative, imaginative, bold undertakings seeking to update this memory and make it compatible with present-day needs.

The results of this fifteen-year accumulation of projects is truly fascinating, and anyone interested may access them through the publicspace.org website. Furthermore, this is why we are presenting this publication: first of all, because it is not a simple accumulation of particular projects, but rather a showcase for trends, groups and shared horizons. Secondly, the sum of these projects helps to preserve the most valuable roots of European cities and to avoid all real-estate temptations or the lure of nostalgia by continually bringing them up to date. Precisely, perhaps, because this is what European cities are: memory and novelty. And maybe, at the end of the day, this is also the best feature of European culture, the culture that might take as its catchphrase the words of one of Catalonia's leading avant-garde poets, Josep Vicenç Foix: "I am exalted by the new, enamored of the old."

**Vicenç Villatoro.** Writer, journalist and Director of the Center of Contemporary Culture of Barcelona (CCCB).

A Northern Perspective

# Juulia Kauste

SUOMEN ARKKITEHTUURIMUSEO, HELSINKI

The Museum of Finnish Architecture has been involved in the European Prize for Urban Public Space since 2006, a welcome opportunity to reflect on the spatial urban context of architecture beyond buildings and structures alone. In turn, the Europe City project has allowed us to deepen our understanding of what is unique about the northern experience and how it contributes to the rich cultural heritage that forms the basis of a shared European identity.

This specificity can be seen in two predominant aspects of our public spaces. First, the climate, with its relatively long, dark, cold winters, makes it necessary to create indoor spaces for people to gather together. Public buildings such as schools and libraries, as well as churches—regardless of a person's religious affiliation— are open to all and are designed to include communal spaces that offer places where the local communities may hold meetings and events. These buildings serve as platforms for a variety of activities initiated by the citizens, thereby facilitating the exchange of ideas through collaboration and working and enjoying life together.

The second characteristic peculiar to the northern experience is how nature constitutes an important part of shared space, even in the urban context. Finland is a case in point. Its abundant shoreline areas and the archipelago that extends along the coasts of the major cities are now accessible thanks to the creation of bicycle paths, ferry connections and the opening up of areas that were formerly the property of the military or industry.

Both of these tendencies—providing schools, libraries and churches as places where people can come together on the common ground of a shared space, as well as the appreciation of natural spaces as something to be made accessible to all—have deep roots in the cultural tradition of Finland. They are also expressions of a readiness to innovatively adjust to the needs of the people in a specific cultural and geographic context, and at the same time to respond to the opportunities that arise and the challenges we face today.

**Juulia Kauste.** Sociologist and Director of the Museum of Finnish Architecture (MFA), Helsinki.

# The New Dynamics of Public Spaces

# Matevž Čelik

MUZEJ ZA ARHITEKTURO IN OBLIKOVANJE, LJUBLJANA

At the Museum of Architecture and Design in Ljubljana we are constantly asking ourselves how meaningful our work is. What is the role of the museum in today's society and how can we support people's efforts to create better and more equal living spaces? We are also aware that architects and designers are questioning how they can contribute—as professionals and individuals—to improvements in public space.

More and more critical architectural practices are emerging that address public space with the objective of changing how people relate to each other. And a growing number of projects denotes how planners and developers are using processes that create conditions for the future physical transformation of spaces. These are projects focused on the regeneration of neglected everyday spaces; on their reorganization and possible new uses. The aim is to initiate change that goes beyond the physical appearance of these interventions and emphasizes the growing interest in the discourse about public space as one of the key political issues of our time.

It is increasingly important to understand how people are using, changing, occupying and defending public space. We have seen how the web and digital communication allow almost endless possibilities for people to connect and have an impact on public space. There are significant results from projects that are making public space in a new way, such as: "do-it-yourself" (DIY) and "do-it-with others" (DIWO). In this way, many small projects can be implemented and become catalysts for impact on a larger scale. Tensions between politics and public-space planning are being exceeded by the self-organization of citizens, social interaction and new ways of production. Through the Europe City project, we were able to research these new dynamics of public space and hopefully contribute to a better understanding of the struggles behind the projects, which will lead to more and better public spaces in the future.

Matevž Čelik. Architect and Director of the Museum of Architecture and Design (MAO), Ljubljana.

# Public Life on the Edges

# Ellis Woodman

THE ARCHITECTURE FOUNDATION, LONDON

In his classic book on the British capital, *London: The Unique City* (1937), Steen Eiler Rasmussen defined the Georgian square as being "a restricted whole, as complete as the courtyard of a convent," a description that points to a fundamental difference between the type and the public squares of continental Europe. Rather than a space of congregation, the British square is essentially a buffer between residential properties. Since the late-nineteenth century Georgian Bloomsbury has been accessible to all, but it was built as a gated community.

Influenced by the achievements of cities like Barcelona, London has made significant progress over the past twenty years in developing a culture of hard landscaping. However, its truly democratic public realm remains the great nineteenth century parks, which Rasmussen valued as "the ideal place for an outdoor life," open to Londoners from every step of the social ladder.

Faced with an estimated increase in population of 1.5 million over the next fifteen years, London is currently embarking on a significant densification of its periphery amidst debate over whether the Metropolitan Greenbelt—the band of open ground that has curtailed London's development since 1935—should remain sacrosanct. What ever the outcome of that discussion, it is clear that access to open land remains an essential requirement of urban life, presenting the urgent need for a new generation of London parks. The city's peripheral growth has already prompted significant investment in opening former sites of industrial and military occupation to public use, as was the case with both the Queen Elizabeth II Olympic Park and Peter Beard_LANDROOM's transformation of Rainham Marshes, which recived a Special Mention in the 2014 edition of the Prize. A central challenge presented by many such projects is the need to incorporate existing functions and infrastructure. The bucolic image presented by London's historic parks is neither attainable nor arguably desirable in these outer London locations. Engulfed by new development, the public spaces of the periphery can offer a precious register of the city's history prior to its regeneration.

**Ellis Woodman.** Architecture critic and Director of The Architecture Foundation (AF), London.

"Public space is the intrinsic element that binds the European urban experience together."

# The Imperfect Idea

## Diane Gray

Public spaces in Europe have long been the scenarios where society's collective framework has been given expression: where history is made and everyday life is played out. Today this continues to be so. The occupation of streets, parks and squares reclaims the role of public space as the places for political demonstration and democratic participation. But public space also provides the places for neighborhood parties and celebrations; for quiet strolls, and for watching the world go by.

Different climates, languages, customs and histories distinguish European countries from one another. The wide variety of public spaces from region to region reflects these differences. At the same time, public space is the intrinsic element that binds the European urban experience together. Public space is the universal feature of the European city. Indeed, the roots of European civilization have been sown in its public spaces from the very beginning. In the transition from the twentieth to the twenty-first centuries we have seen an exponential growth of this tradition, which has been the basis of the European Prize for Urban Public Space since it was established in 2000 by the Center for Contemporary Culture of Barcelona.

The objective of this book is to present a multifaceted and diverse platform of ideas about European public space and its social, cultural and economic significance. This discussion is approached from different disciplines, resulting in a wide-ranging reflection about the diversity of public spaces across the continent.

The first part of this book focuses on what has been learned through the sum of the European experience. The seven essays that focus on these "lessons" contain many references to the past, to the concepts of the *agora* and the *polis*, and to the historical importance of the city in the construction of European culture. At the same time, in the form of the fifty-four projects that accompany the lessons we see that while the contemporary social agenda continues to address these concepts, it also raises new questions and experiments with new answers. These projects have been carried out over the last fifteen years, thereby providing another reading that traces the development of ideas and strategies and allows for an analysis of recent production and future possibilities in terms of the formal and functional aspects of public spaces across the continent.

The second part of the book begins with a brief, recent history of European public space that contextualizes the entire discussion. Subsequently, four essays talk about the interdependence of our shared histories and cultures throughout our ever-increasingly small planet. The opinions of professionals living and working outside of Europe allow for reflections on our similarities and our differences, and encourage an interchange of experiences and ideas coming from a perspective that is much wider than that coming only from Europe.

Josep Lluís Sert, himself a multidisciplinary professional who worked all over the world as an architect and urban designer, made it his lifelong mission to investigate the close relationship between urban life and public space. After emigrating from Barcelona—the city from which this Prize is organized—to the United States, as Dean he established the first urban design program at the Graduate School of Design (GSD) of Harvard University. In his 1942 publication he famously asked "Can our Cities Survive?" And nearly forty years later, he was still asking questions about and seeking answers for how urban form can respond to the complex necessities of our time:

"The current architectural idiom is subject, even more than before, to urban conditions, urban vocabulary, and urban design. Our buildings depend increasingly on what is around them: congestion, high densities, access, parking facilities, etc. The physical conditions of the environment determine such designs. As we look around and see what is happening with cities and human settlements in the world, and how many of the good things are being ignored and even destroyed, we should ask ourselves: 'is our culture and technological prowess incapable of building a more balanced environment?'"

Sert's observations and his question are as relevant today as they were in the early 1980s. This book forms part of this continuous process of questions and answers, of proposals and experiments, and aspires to contribute to the ongoing development of a European urban project based on quality of life and equality for all, where public space is the common denominator.

So perhaps one of the most important values that the European urban model embodies is its desire and its capacity to "keep going" despite serious historical reverses, not least of which was the reconstruction of much of the continent after the two world wars of the last century. Perhaps Europe has learned that it is not so much about the answers, but about the questions, which are raised again and again. Questions that are based on a long process of "trial and error," of getting back up and persisting in working on the imperfect idea that the city will always be.

# LESS

# ONS

**FROM THE EUROPEAN PRIZE
FOR URBAN PUBLIC SPACE**

"What remains of the old European model of the city? What can Europe contribute to the world through its cities? What is singular about the European city today?"

# Public Space and Democracy

## Judit Carrera

The form of the city is intimately linked with democracy. This is the basic premise of the European Prize for Urban Public Space which, since it was first awarded in 2000, the CCCB has presided over in partnership with several prominent European institutions working in the domain of architecture. The Prize has now become a permanent observatory of European cities and, every two years, receives more than three hundred entries of noteworthy projects aiming to trans form and improve public spaces which, the length and breadth of the continent, highlight the relational and collective nature of typically urban settings.

Public spaces are specific, delimited, physical places but, if they are important, it is primarily because they are also immaterial spaces with considerable political potential. The city is the place where some of the most basic principles of democracy are identified, expanded, and challenged.

First of all, an ideal public space is a zone of free, universal access, which is to say open and without any excluding fences or walls. Accordingly, the principle of equality is consubstantial with urban public space which, if it is to be truly democratic, should not discriminate against anyone on grounds of origin, class or race. Yet this is not simply a matter of equality of access. It also, and especially, entails *performative* equality. In being open to everyone, public spaces are able to distribute resources, power and imaginaries and, in doing so, make the city more democratic.

The second principle enshrined in the concept of public space is freedom of expression. The city is an intermediate space between individual and state, a place where criticism of power is encouraged and civil society is reinforced by freely circulating ideas. Civil and political rights are conquered in public spaces which, even today and for all the technological innovations that have created virtual public spheres, are gathering places *par excellence* where political protest and demands may be expressed. Public places therefore aspire to be zones of free words and movement, in which people will not encounter censorship or find barriers in their way.

If the city has always been a potential setting for the peaceful coexistence of strangers, today's public spaces face the challenge of welcoming, safeguarding and strengthening the growing pluralism of European societies. A truly democratic public space is one which, in its design and in its use, stimulates a sense of belonging to a wider community beyond the bounds of the strictly private sphere. It is, then, a milieu that fosters contact between different people, mixing uses and populations and preventing the formation of ghettos. Like democracy, public space is a meeting place for individual and collective interests, where "I" and "us" come together. In short, it is a space where the common good is forged.

Precisely because individual and collective interests do not always coincide, public space is essentially a locus of discord. It is far from being a paradise. On the contrary, it is an ambivalent place which, although having great democratic potential, is also both a location and mirror of the most crucial social conflicts. As a result of the present pace of growth and transformation in contemporary cities, coexistence and survival are now jeopardized by injustice and irresponsibility. However, in cities, as nowhere else, opportunities for democracy and sustainability also flourish. The European Prize for Urban Public Space is fully located within this contradiction and, in becoming thus a privileged witness to the most serious problems of European cities, it has also been able to contribute examples of improvements and solutions.

## Unity and Diversity

This book draws attention to seven of the great areas in which the democratic health of cities in Europe is at stake: the different and frequently clashing memories coexisting in a city; problems of mobility and the prevalence, even today, of the private car; urban complexity and the mixture of uses and populations; peripheries and the physical limits of cities; seafronts and riverfronts, scenes of collective identity and of access to water as part of the public good; markets and new forms of production and consumption in the postindustrial city; and democracy and the ways in which citizens appropriate public space. Each theme comes with an essay by a writer or thinker in the domain of urban theory and is illustrated by several outstanding works presented for the European Prize for Urban Public Space. This is no closed list of normative vocation, but an invitation to discuss themes which, as the experience of fifteen years of observation through the Prize has revealed, mark the existence of European cities today.

Most of these issues are intrinsic to urban life and, as such, are not necessarily new although, nowadays, they appear in particularly acute or revamped forms. One example is the problem of how to deal with the tyranny of the private car. If, in the 1980s, the response was mainly to pedestrianize old city centers, priority attention focuses at present on peripheral areas, fruit of the urban sprawl which is now a predominant feature of the continent's metropolitan regions. Neither is historic memory a new phenomenon. Since the end of the Second World War, many European cities have been working to acknowledge old wounds in their public spaces and to display measures subsequently taken towards reconciliation with their past. The demolition of the Berlin Wall, the end of Soviet-style regimes, and the scars of the Spanish Civil War are all historic phenomena which, translated into different forms, seek to be represented in their respective urban spaces across the continent. Then again, urban peripheries, the most overlooked spaces of cities, have nowadays become mirrors of new kinds of segregation in Europe. In recent years we have also witnessed a proliferation of citizens' initiatives which, appropriating public space, have called for more democratic cities and governments.

All of these matters are persistently manifested all over Europe and, while they might be concentrated in a variety of ways in some European cities, in keeping with local traditions or geographic conditions, they also shape a certain shared imaginary of the challenges faced today by the modern European city model.

## The Singularity of Europe

Like the Prize, this book takes as its starting point the hypothesis that one of Europe's greatest contributions to the world is its particular way of understanding and experiencing the city. With its origins in ancient Greece, European civilization flowered in the city where the core principles of democracy also developed. In their history, form and diversity, the cities of Europe are one of the most characteristic features of the continent's identity and, even today, constitute one of the world's most sustainable examples of urban habitat. Unlike megalopolises in other parts of the world, they are distinctive for their human scale and in having a dense, complex structure which is notable for its mixed uses and populations. Moreover, European cities, many of them millenarian, are the result of an overlapping of different historical layers which coexist more or less harmoniously. This dense, complex form of the European city and its condition as a palimpsest of layers of history foster the coexistence of different social and cultural strata in its public spaces. Today, however, this model is at risk because of unchecked urban growth, gentrification, new forms of racism and xenophobia, bad urban planning, unsustainable practice, and widespread urban and social segregation, all of which are incompatible with the democratic principles inherent to public space.

What remains of the old European city model? What can Europe contribute to the world through its cities? What is singular about the European city today? In order to respond to these questions, we have asked several thinkers from Europe and beyond to cast a critical eye on the specificity of European urban form, with particular attention to cross-cutting histories, and the connections and tensions between Europe and the rest of the world. This is a detached gaze, through which it is possible to highlight the strengths and weaknesses of a model that urgently needs to be reinvented.

This fifteen-year study of public space appeals for humility from a continent which keeps raising walls, thus betraying its own principles, and calls for a more democratic, plural and essentially cosmopolitan Europe. The European Prize for Urban Public Space has its origins in a steadfast defense of the founding principles of the European city. Applying self-criticism, as befits the continent's Enlightenment legacy, it seeks to contribute towards renewing this time-honored model by means of learning from the good practices which, across the continent, reveal that a better city is possible.

**Judit Carrera.** Director of the European Prize for Urban Public Space.

Places for the collective memory have long been a part of the European city. In the latter part of the twentieth century we have seen how the concept of the monument has been redefined as an interactive, educational and emotional public space.

Mem

"What if the city kept all the actions, discourses and thoughts of its inhabitants? Would there still be space left for the city?"

# Memory and City: What Does a City Conserve?

## A Philosophical Approach

# Gonçalo M. Tavares

*It is evident that material constructions are not immortal, they're things that fade away just the same, only more slowly:*

*"If you ask: 'Why is Thekla's [city] construction taking such a long time?' the inhabitants [...] reply: 'So that its destruction cannot begin.'"*

Italo Calvino, *Invisible Cities*

### Action, Thought and Discourse (An Approach from Arendt)

*What can a city keep in a museum, in a warehouse?*
*The answer is not that evident.*

Action, discourse and thought in themselves "neither produce nor generate anything, they are as futile as life itself. In order to become worldly things, that is, deeds and facts and events and patterns of thought or ideas, they must first be seen, heard, and remembered, and then transformed, 'reified' [...]."[1]

Action, discourse and thought do not produce things, matter with volume which occupies space: they are elements that drift between appearance and disappearance; when they appear in the world they disappear from the world, unlike a stone. In fact, when faced with a stone observers, having verified its existence, may close their eyes

---

1 "Action, the only activity that goes on directly between men without the intermediary of things or matter." Hannah Arendt, *The Human Condition*. (Chicago: The University of Chicago Press, 1958), 7.

and reopen them safe in the knowledge that the stone will still be there. The one who speaks, on the other hand, does something without using matter that will remain in the world. What was spoken disappeared; what was thought disappeared—and in this case, let's say, it is a *private disappearance*—only the thinker himself may declare "I don't know where that which I thought has gone." On the contrary, when one speaks or acts this can be contemplated, others may testify to it,[2] and in that sense there is an *us* who can say: "we do not know where what you said is anymore," or: "we do not know where the deed you performed is anymore." The only separation between thought, action and discourse lies in the potential existence of witnesses other than oneself. Thought has no witnesses. What all three have in common, therefore, is the fact that they are immaterial.

*What if the city kept all the actions, discourses and thoughts of its inhabitants? Would there still be space left for the city?*

## Things and Actions: Extinction and Importance of Memory

Note that worldly things—either immobile, like a stone, or mobile, like a horse—are things which materially persist in this world; they can therefore be sought and found. Only a conscious, cogent method of destruction can make a concrete worldly thing disappear. Thus, *no longer seeing an action* and *no longer seeing a horse* are two different things. The horse that disappeared from our field of vision can be sought: *if it disappeared, that's because it's somewhere else.* On the other hand, the action that disappeared from our field of vision *cannot be sought, it is not somewhere else*; in fact it *no longer exists.* And only if we call nonexistence *somewhere else* and use **memory** as the instrument for seeking what no longer exists—in this case, the past—shall we be able to regard an action or a sentence *as being a thing.* What existed and no longer does is *in memory's perspective still a thing*: only memory can make it present.

Arendt writes: "Without remembrance, and without the reification which remembrance needs for its own consummation and which, as the Greeks held, actually makes it the mother of all the arts,

---

2 "Action, as distinguished from fabrication, is never possible in isolation; to be isolated is to be deprived of the capacity to act. Action and discourse need the surrounding presence of others no less than fabrication needs the surrounding presence of nature for its material, and of a world, in which to place the finished product." She later adds: "Since action acts upon beings who are capable of their own actions, reaction, apart from being a response, is always a new action that strikes out on its own and affects others." According to Arendt, action can thus only exist in the city, in a collective (op. cit., 190).

the living activities of action, discourse, and thought would lose their reality at the end of each process and disappear as if they had never existed."[3] Very important, therefore, is the fact that "we are surrounded by things more permanent than the activity by which they were produced, and potentially even more permanent than the lives of their authors." For example, to read Seneca's *Moral Letters to Lucilius*, written almost two thousand years ago, is to stand before the astonishing imbalance between the countless hours Seneca invested in writing it—which we cannot see and shall never see since they ceased to exist at the time when they existed—and the twenty centuries throughout which the thing, the outcome of an *ephemeral muscular activity* (writing), has lasted as a contemplable object.

In this sense, there is a potential hierarchy of activities, which may be valued in accordance with *the durability of the things* they generate. In short, an activity is the more valuable the longer things originated by it last. But such a formula entails several problems: in the case of amorous acts, for example, a simple kiss soon disappears.

## Food and Art: Conservation and City

The least durable of all things is food, as Arendt reminds us, quoting Locke. Food is something indispensable to the survival of mankind, a thing which, "if not consumed by use will decay and perish by itself."[4] Food is therefore subject to the fastest cycle of appearance-disappearance. The length of time that elapses between when it is placed in the world and the moment when it deteriorates and disappears is minimal. Food is a thing (neither an action nor a discourse, evidently); a thing, indeed, yet it bears within itself *a self-destruction capacity* (capacity or fault, depending on how you look at it): it exists to be consumed and, once consumed, immediately disappears.

Compare, for example, the difference between bread, an apple, and a table or other man-made object. There is—one can feel it—a certain obsession with how long things made by man will last. The table has to last, the building has to last; and works of art, in this field, being a kind of *useless architecture, craft without practical use*, their greatest utility lies precisely in their durability. Art's usefulness, one might say, is proportional to how long it lasts. And in this context, it will occupy the number-one position among the things made by humans. Taken to the extreme, the most important thing made by mankind will be the one that comes closest to maximum durability, to immortality.

## Life Span and City

When setting to work, and by virtue of his initial selection of materials and processes, the artisan may decide whether to make an object that will last three or three hundred years. This individual human decision[5] is a decision that, in a way, claims for itself one of the acts attributed exclusively, since time immemorial, to natural and "divine" making. The prophecies that the gods *blew* into the ear of certain privileged people about someone's life span and the causes of his or her death are a good example of this. Knowing the date of one's death—that is, one's own life span—is *nonhuman knowledge*; therefore, the fact that man may know the life span of a certain thing made by himself is of great importance to man. Not only the gods may now *promise time*; man may also do this. The artisan promises that the object he made—in normal circumstances, excluding catastrophes—will last for centuries, and the customer will buy it in this hope.

And so we face another fundamental question: in the act of making, selling, and buying lies the essence of the city. Only things *that last longer than a human life span* are made, sold or bought, for man invented a collective way to become immortal, namely the city. We inevitably come, therefore, to the question of the common world, of public space, on which Arendt elaborates so well:

"Only the existence of a public realm and the world's subsequent transformation into a community of things which gathers men together and relates them to each other depends entirely on permanence. If the world is to contain a public space, it cannot be erected for one generation and planned for the living only; it must transcend the life span of mortal men."[6]

Scale ceases therefore to be an individual human being, his or her life span and mortality, to become *Man*, with his collective life and its great durability.

---

5 Anselm, one of Musil's characters, says "You must make a decision. That is not a thought, Maria. To decide: as if you, in the most immaterial darkness, would close your admirable hand and, suddenly, felt something in it, like an unexpected, magnificent body!" (Robert Musil, *The Visionaries*).

6 Arendt, op. cit., 55.

Arendt continues, "Without this transcendence into a potential earthly immortality, no politics, in the strict sense, no common world and no public realm would be possible."

Only human beings may thus conceive what is between them; which will not be part exclusively of a single life: "the common world is what we enter when we are born and what we leave behind when we die."

*It is this common world, a world of city and memory, that separates mankind from the rest of nature; that separates the human being from other animals.*

*The human being as the only animal that uses the previous generation's memories.*

Text written and adapted from fragments of the author's book *Atlas do Corpo e da Imaginação* [Atlas of the Body and of the Imagination], (Alfragide: Caminho, 2013).

**Gonçalo M. Tavares.** Writer, playwright and poet. Author of *Jerusalem* (2005) and *Atlas do Corpo e da Imaginação* (2013).

# Huéscar
Spain
**Tower of Homage**
Antonio Jiménez Torrecillas
Special Mention 2008

Located near the unstable border between the Islamic and Christian realms, the medieval town of Huéscar built a watchtower in order to monitor the surrounding territory. When the hostilities came to an end, its wooden upper structure was dismantled, while the stone base eventually merged with neighboring houses. At the beginning of the twenty-first century, with the project of recovering the monument, there were no documents describing exactly how it had been built. It was therefore decided to build the upper wooden structure in a contemporary language. Rather than imitating the original form, the new construction has restored its predecessor's functions of landmark and lookout.

# Zadar

Croatia

**Renovation of the Petar Zoranić Square**

Aleksandra Krebel, Alan Kostrenčić

**Finalist 2014**

Extensive bombing during the Yugoslav Wars made it necessary to totally restore this central square in the historic center. In addition to the valuable buildings that are located there, it is also the site of significant Roman and medieval ruins. One of the primary objectives of the project was to ensure the coexistence of the ruins with contemporary life and, in fact, to allow for visual contact between the two. Like windows looking into the past, sheets of glass have been installed over the ruins permitting unobstructed movement across the square.

# Krakow
Poland

**Heroes of the Ghetto Square**
Biuro Projektow Lewicki Latak,
Piotr Lewicki & Kazimierz Latak
**Special Mention 2006**

Known by the Nazis as Umschlagplatz, the old Zgody Square was the point where Jews from the Krakow ghetto had to gather before being deported. The belongings they brought with them kept piling up and they were forced to abandon them before their last journey to the concentration camps. Sixty years later, an artistic intervention placing a series of weathering-steel chairs around the square rescued this horrendous past from oblivion. Their dreamlike air evokes the household belongings abandoned in public space, and brings the memory of absent people back to the present.

# Nantes
### France

**Memorial to the Abolition of Slavery**
Wodiczko + Bonder, architecture, art & design
Special Mention 2012

In the eighteenth century, the river port of Nantes was the main departure point for French slave-trading expeditions. The slave ships docked at the Quai de la Fosse on the right bank of the Loire River which, until recently, had fallen into neglect. It was used as a parking lot and lacked any reference to its gruesome past. When the wharf was converted into a riverside walk, its triangular support structure, recalling a ship's hold, was used to house a museum which presents the history of slavery and the struggles against it.

## La campagne négrière

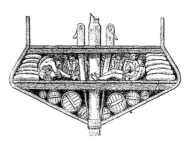

*Vue en coupe d'un navire négrier.*
Gravure (d'après une aquarelle de Bernardin de Saint-Pierre)
tirée de « Nouveaux faits relatifs à la traite des Noirs »,
édité par la Société de la Morale Chrétienne, 1826.
Bibliothèque des Musées du Château des Ducs de Bretagne.
Cliché Anneaux de la Mémoire.

# Barcelona
Spain

**Restoration of the Turó de la Rovira**
Jansana, de la Villa, de Paauw arquitectes,
AAUP Jordi Romero i associats,
History of the City Museum
**Joint Winner 2012**

Despite its magnificent views, the peak of the Turó de la Rovira was a neglected, not very accessible and little-known place. As such, it hid the remains of anti-aircraft gun emplacements, Barcelona's defense against Fascist bombing attacks during the Spanish Civil War, and also the shanty dwellings that were built over them in subsequent decades. These vestiges, which recall the ravages of war and express the difficulties of finding adequate housing, were carefully restored in a project that has also made the site more accessible. Now, besides being a popular lookout, it also teaches visitors about the city's recent history.

# Kalmar

Sweden

**Stortorget**
Caruso St John Architects, Eva Löfdahl
**Special Mention 2004**

The history of Kalmar is inscribed in the cobblestone paving of Stortorget, the city's main square. The same large, rough-hewn stones had raised walls around the edges of the square and, later, the walls of houses, as well as paving the streets. By the 1980s, however, the square had been downgraded to the status of parking lot and the paving was irreversibly damaged by the zones of circulation marked off within it. Once the private vehicle was banned from Stortorget, the paving in the square was renovated and the city's past now resonates therein.

# Berlin

Germany

## Tilla Durieux Park

Jana Crepon, Bruno Doedens, Ingo Golz, Merijn Groenhart, Harma Horlings, Willem Jan Snel, Maike van Stiphout, DS Landschapsarchitecten
**Special Mention 2004**

During the construction boom of the 1990s many of the empty spaces surrounding the length of the Berlin Wall were either used as building sites or neglected. Falling into the latter category, the Prachtgleis, a five-hundred-meters-long esplanade, linking Potsdamer Platz with the Land-wehrkanal and flanked on either side by rows of residential and other buildings, resembled a large vacant lot. The addition of two big grassy slopes transformed the space into a popular green space, much like a beach, which saved it from real-estate voracity while also conserving the memory of the old wound of the wall.

# Altach

Austria

**Islamic Cemetery**
Bernardo Bader Architects
Special Mention 2014

Although Austria was a pioneer in Europe in recognizing the religious freedoms of Muslims, there wa
only one Islamic cemetery in the country before 2012. Located in the federal state where Austria'
largest concentration of Muslims resides, the town of Altach wished to provide another such facil
ity, which combines contemporary architecture with highly specific installations in order to satisf
ablution rites and other requirements. Islam is a religion that is closely bound with the history o
Europe. Now believers have a place where they can bury their dead and remember them in their new
homeland, contributing to a feeling of connection with the rest of the community.

After more than a decade of large-scale demolition and extensive building, the construction of a big shopping mall in the center of Folkestone changed the urban landscape to the point of alienating the residents' sense of belonging. The initiative "Other People's Photographs" entailed the collection of thousands of images of everyday street scenes accumulated over the years. Printed on metal supports and installed in the places where they were taken, the images interwove the personal memories that the people shared, thus fostering the recovery of collective memory and helping to reconstruct the bonds between the social and urban fabrics.

Mobility is a fundamental issue in the contemporary city. Access to and exclusion from public transport have huge social and economic implications. On the other hand, solutions are being implemented to encourage systems of movement that offset the pervasive use of the individual car.

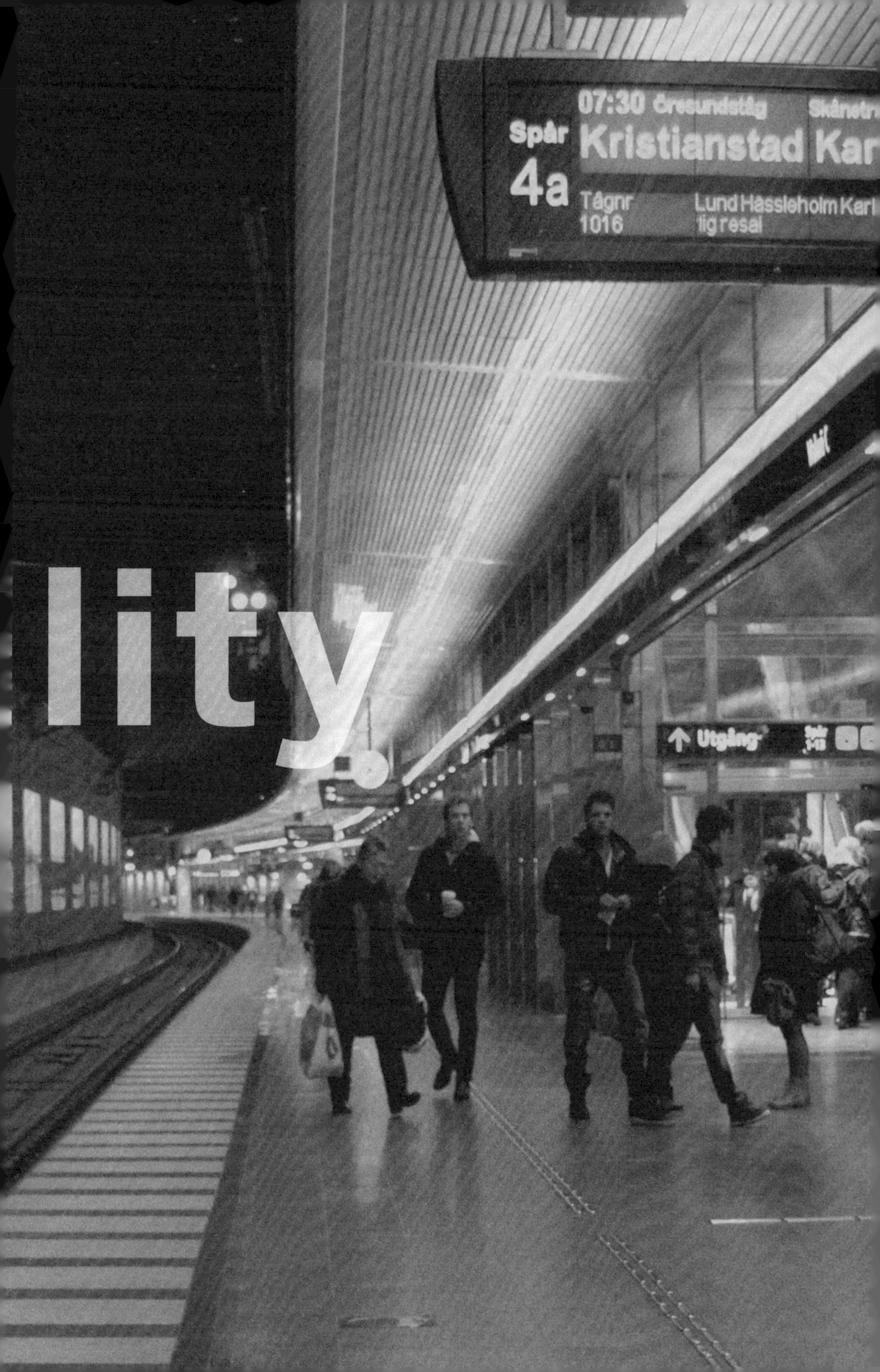
lity
Spår
4a
07:30
Kristianstad
Tågnr
1016
Utgång

"To my mind, the city is a space where we can move around or just hang out, build relationships and have unexpected adventures."

# Walking the Edge
## Francesco Careri

I can definitely lay no claim to being an expert when it comes to mobility, whether it's pedestrian, cycling, vehicular or infrastructural. It's more the "going" that interests me—not so much as a practical and functional act to help solve those space-time mobility challenges, but rather as a poetic and non-functional practice that often ends up complicating those very challenges with its myriad of experiences. I'm profoundly convinced that "it is when we waste time that we gain space" and it's more fun trying to divert people off their chosen pathways and away from their goals than helping them achieve them. But if that makes sense to me as an intellectual, artist and peripatetic teacher, it has less meaning if I happen to be late, or stuck in traffic, if I'm worrying about what will happen to my children when they go off on their first walk on their own, crossing the road at traffic lights that no-one takes any notice of, when they take their bikes into places with no bike lanes. So I'm going to take advantage of this opportunity to try to reconcile the two different people inside me. One loves getting lost, tries to catch the city unawares by slipping off down its backstreets and alleyways, whereas the other has trains to catch, schedules and appointments to keep and places to get to as quickly as possible. Two different parts of me, two parts of all of us, each with different space and time at our disposal, not just in the sense of the physical spaces we travel through or the clocks that tick away relentlessly beside us, but also of our desires, at any given time, to meet other people at our leisure.

To my mind, the city is a space where we can move around or just hang out, build relationships and have unexpected adventures. But then I start to wonder: in smartphone city, where everyone walks around plugged into headphones, answering work e-mails and chatting on social networks, is there still room in our hearts for places for interaction like the ones I'm talking about? Does anyone still want leisure time? Do we still need meeting places? Yes, of course we do because, even if they do have smartphones implanted into their brains and under their skin, we still want the next generations to be able to carry on crossing at junctions, cycling around and staying out late in the evening fooling around with their friends. And it's far from a foregone conclusion. In today's Europe, we can still do all these things, but the rest of the world can't.

Here, despite the best efforts of the media and politicians, security mania hasn't yet taken hold. And, thank goodness, the space we have for "going" still manages to accommodate various different speeds and provides more opportunities to meet Otherness. It has to carry on being a space both for discovery, leisure and meeting people, and for the indifference of folks in a hurry who have no time to get distracted by what's going on around them. Faster flows have to be able to coexist with slower ones, with those of people in cars, on bicycles and on benches. But most of all, our cities have to cater for the flows of the beautiful, good and kind alongside those of the "ugly, dirty and bad," as the title of a famous 1970s Italian movie goes. As designers of train stations and airports well know, spaces for mobility also need to be places for idling away our time and meeting people, which is why they put in bars, restaurants and shopping malls to make sure we turn our spare time into time for consumption and shopping. This model, which sociologists explained some twenty-odd years ago, is gradually taking over all of our urban space, and it increasingly tends to exclude Otherness in all its forms: the ugly (i.e. the different or the poor— but at least with a European passport), the dirty (usually the foreigner or Roma—whether nomadic or sedentary) and the bad (not just the thief or drug dealer, but also all forms of organized conflict, such as civic movements claiming rights to the city, to life, to homes, to jobs). People who are increasingly being shut out of the city, forcibly thrown out or simply put off by the costs of living, a double-edged sword used to try to prevent even visual contact with citizen-consumers, a dying breed in the spaces used for mobility.

At airports, once we get through baggage control this design has run riot, the old six-seater train compartment today is reserved for impoverished commuters in the slower regions, whereas people on the move want expensive seats where they can open up their laptops and carry on working without wasting any precious time. Trams, buses and metros are the only means that still allow promiscuity, proximity, physical contact, unexpected encounters, a minimal dose of danger and experience. But only for those who can still afford the fare. Otherness gets there on foot. Outside Europe, indeed, walkers are identified as being homeless, thieves or potential murderers. At each street corner in rich neighborhoods we are spied on by useless surveillance cameras, which may be able to reconstruct the dynamics in a video but can't deter or stop your attackers. That doesn't mean we need the army on the streets, like many politicians claim, but we need more human eyes, more bodies, more social skills. We need more people walking around on the streets. We need to find out how to make walking areas both more adventurous when we have time to kill and faster when we're in a hurry—only then will they be even safer: more people out on the streets means more security, that's a truism. We're not asking that much, but the world is going in the wrong direction. In São Paulo in Brazil, the rich are hardly ever even seen at street level. From their apartments, they go up onto their terraces and climb into their helicopters, while their chauffeurs take their children to the university where they sit in the classroom surrounded by bodyguards— I've seen them. But even in the new urban sprawl, home to the European middle classes, things are not much better. There are whole new areas that can only be accessed by car and the people who live there extend the private space of their homes to their offices, via their garages, traveling ensconced inside the mobile armor of their cars to yet another garage at the shopping mall or office. In such lives, places where we get to rub up against Otherness, like the newsdealer's, the baker's, the tobacconist's, the bus stop, have all but disappeared. So even when we are on the move, we live inside non-communicating bubbles, self-referential mobile islands.

The metaphor of the archipelago as a narrative of European metropolises is now almost universally accepted—a sea of voids, inlets and cavities, at times well preserved such as parkland or farmland, at others abandoned such as pastures and *terrains vagues*, open spaces separating islands of different sizes such as neighborhoods, enclaves, gated communities, industrial areas, Roma camps, slums: homogeneous islands, unconnected with each other and often lacking even the fast mobility of rail networks. The outer forgotten islands, especially the poorer ones, as well as having no safe routes also lack open areas, meeting spaces, gardens, and there's no more space available to create them. In such cases, the metaphor of the archipelago comes to our aid. We can work on the edges that in maritime parlance would be our seafronts. Very often it's along the edges that there's room, all it takes is a few meters for a pavement to become a bike lane, to become a venue for sport, shade, seating, minor services, trees, gardens, *terrains vagues*, until they turn into linear parks, linear town squares often bordered by abandoned natural sites which with a little care could be rejuvenated, so that its slums can be replaced by social campsites where tourists live in tents side by side with the homeless, areas where Otherness can proudly manifest its diversity, as used to happen with circuses in marginal spaces in towns the world over. Along the edges there are still adventures to experience. And it's at the edges that paths can begin, crossing the sea and in just a few minutes getting to metro stations where as often as not parking spaces are at a premium and getting there by car can take hours. On the edges we can imagine docks, piers, seafronts, marinas, beaches, ports … kilometers of coastline where the sea of Otherness, the Nomad's desert and Migrants' boats can berth and establish a dialogue with old, worn-out Mother Europe.

**Francesco Careri.** Architect. Professor in the Department of Urban Studies at the Università degli Studi Roma Tre. Author of *Walkscapes: Walking as an Aesthetic Practice* (2002).

# Helsinki
## Finland
### Baana Pedestrian and Bicycle Corridor
Helsinki City Planning Department, Helsinki Public
Works Department, Loci Landscape Architects
### Special Mention 2014

In 2008, the cargo port of Länsisatama was demolished with the result that the freight train running to the central station became obsolete. The railway left a gash in the urban fabric but covering it is an expensive option and will take time. Meanwhile, the space has been temporarily turned over to cyclists and pedestrians as a track with garden patches and imbued with the atmosphere of the old railway line. Austere, versatile and resistant, this recycling of the old railway is the result of a cooperative effort between the administration, academics and residents in a process of provisional urban planning that preserves the industrial memory while opening up the way to sustainable alternatives for mobility.

# Teruel

Spain

**Refurbishment of the Paseo del Óvalo**
David Chipperfield Architects, b720
Arquitectos, Fermín Vázquez
**Joint Winner 2004**

The old center of Teruel crowns a promontory which ends abruptly in a seventeen-meter-high retaining wall. A Mudejar-style imperial stairway links the Paseo de Óvalo on top of the wall with the railway station square at the bottom. With the advent of the high-speed train, lifts were installed to supplement the stairway and bring access to the town center and the station up to present-day standards. This required opening up a large hole not unlike an entrance to a walled city. Far from mere functionality, the new infrastructure achieves a degree of monumentality that is worthy of its companion, the old stairway.

# Dublin
Ireland
## Smithfield Esplanade
McGarry Ní Éanaigh Architects
Joint Winner 2000

A majestic open space in medieval Dublin, the Smithfield esplanade played a key role in the city's activity until the nineteenth century when the livestock market was moved elsewhere. The subsequent invasion by private vehicles only aggravated its decline. Once it was cleared of parked cars in order to create an exclusively pedestrian zone, the original paving was restored and twelve tall street lights were installed, giving the space an even rhythm and visual unity. It has now gone back to being an important public space combining everyday life with its use as a venue for big events.

# Robbiano

Italy

**Black Square, White Square**
Ifdesign, Ida Origgi, Chiara Toscani
Special Mention 2006

The San Quirico and Giulitta churches looked onto a large but underused space with a featureless traffic circle and congested with moving vehicles. In 2005 the council decided to make it the town's main square. In front of the Giulitta church there is now a spread of basalt with two black stone benches, a pool of water and a fountain while, in front of the San Quirico church, steps in white Trani stone fold out to pave an open area. What was once just space has now become a symbolic and functional place for lingering.

Exhibition Road, the site of major cultural and educational facilities, was once crammed with cars, both parked and circulating, which created many obstacles for pedestrians. In 2011, the street was cleared and the traffic reorganized so that pedestrians and vehicles could use the space according to the shared space concept with a reduced speed limit. Besides removing architectural barriers from the street, the intervention opted for versatility over specificity, trusting in a capacity for coexistence between respectful drivers and prudent pedestrians. Exhibition Road now serenely accommodates the diversity of movement associated with a main thoroughfare.

# Malmö
Sweden
## Elsewhere
Tania Ruiz
Special Mention 2012

A large installation has occupied Malmö's Central Station since the city's public transport authorities decided to stop encouraging irresponsible consumption and remove all advertising from the subway. On the two walls flanking the subway line, twenty-five synchronized projections show films taken from moving trains. Hence, the screens, which run along the whole length of the station, look like windows of a railway car in movement, unhurriedly crossing landscapes all over the world. The installation gives poetic sense to waiting on its platforms and, every day, gently persuades 37,000 passengers to opt for public transport over the private car and thereby to diminish air pollution and reduce urban sprawl.

Two abandoned gas stations were located along the highway at the entrance to the new Nooderpark, which was created by fusing together several green areas in Amsterdam North. Instead of demolishing these derelict buildings, the decision was made to take advantage of the open, flat roofs typical of such structures and recycle them to create a new covered public square. Colorful light installations placed under the roofs recall the changing Dutch sky and transform the gas stations into a luminous landmark that can be appreciated by people driving by, cycling or spending time in the park.

# Buenavista del Norte

Spain

**Green Tenerife**
Félix Perera, Urbano Yanes, GPY Arquitectos
**Special Mention 2004**

The urban fabric of Buenavista del Norte abruptly stopped when it reached the Barranco de Triana ravine, which separated the Triana neighborhood from the old town center and obstructed everyday mobility for residents. The implementation of Phase 9 of the "Green Tenerife" Plan, which aimed to address the island's lack of green spaces, improved the connection between both sectors. The ravine became an accessible park with a network of pedestrian paths crossing through it to connect the Plaza de Triana with the Parque de San Francisco and the Plaza del Chorro in the old town center.

This integrated public transport system consists of a train and a rapid city tram that connects the center of Wroclaw with the new stadium on the outskirts of the city. The two stops function on different levels, which are connected by elevators and stairs. The train stop is located on the existing railway line on the ground level with the tram stop on the platform above. A triangular reinforced concrete roof floats over the platform while a wide, monumental ramp directs the large number of people attending the sporting events towards the public square directly opposite the stadium.

**Elx**
Spain

**The Braided Valley**
Francisco Leiva Ivorra,
Marta García Chico,
Antoni Baile Jiménez,
Prócoro del Real Baeza
Joint Winner 2014

ELCHE

In the 1970s, channeling work along the Vinalopó River put an end to flooding but also eliminated the network of paths used by residents on the right bank to reach the nearby Palmeral Park. The watercourse thus became a barrier splitting the city in two until it was converted into a lineal park. Now it is crisscrossed by a network of tracks and footbridges linking both sides of the river and anticipating paths that the common sense of walkers might leave around awkwardly situated parterres. The intervention encourages people to walk between the city's less privileged neighborhoods and the old center.

The European urban model is the compact and complex city. In this sense, mixed-use is the key and the multifunctional city is where the public spaces—streets, squares, markets, and parks—actively integrate these functions.

Mix

ture

*"The complexity of the European city is thus based on a gamble that remains fully valid, that of associating urbanization and urbanity."*

# On Complexity

## Olivier Mongin

Now that the process of urban globalization is presenting us with contrasting scenarios, and while material and immaterial flows are placing territories as a whole under pressure, is the European city about to become "peripheral"? Is Rem Koolhaas not right when he says that African megacities like Lagos are the laboratories of the contemporary city? Without ignoring the rapid transformations now in progress across the planet, it is essential to showcase the European city in all its aspects and to emphasize its complexity. A complexity that goes hand in hand with its dual nature, the association of the *urbs* and the *civitas*, urbanization and urbanity, the relationship between a territory and its inhabitants.

It is true that there is no single historical model of a European city; what we have instead are certain singular European cities. The historian Fernand Braudel stated that there are two urban systems in place in Europe: countries like France give priority to the State and see cities as microstates, whereas countries like Italy uphold the autonomy of cities. Even so, the European city is at the origin of the great sociological literature of the early-twentieth century, the literature influenced by Max Weber, Georg Simmel, and Norbert Elias, the literature that sees the city dweller as the witness of nascent modernity. In any event, the complexity of the urban territories highlighted is the outcome of at least three factors: that which falls within the remit of an urban project; that which is driven by an imaginary; and that which makes a democratic ethos possible at a political level.

### The Urban Project

The word "urbanism" is now universally understood, but it is worth remembering that it did not appear until 1867 in the work of Ildefons Cerdà, who formulated a *General Theory of Urbanization* and imagined the new plan for Barcelona. The invention of urbanism is not, however, historically connected solely with the rise of the industrial city—of which London and Paris, described by Walter Benjamin as the "capital of the nineteenth century," were the chief examples at the time—, as it is inextricably linked to a dual state of spirit that itself stems from two sources. Firstly, urbanism draws on the architectural tradition of the Renaissance, as set out in Alberti's treatise on architecture (*De re aedificatoria*, 1452), and reflects three criteria (*necessitas*, the laws of applied physics and respect for natural balances; *commoditas*, dialogic respect for the client's demands; and *voluptas*, aesthetic pleasure) that remain meaningful today. And secondly, it is inspired by the utopian tradition, as exemplified by Thomas More's *Utopia* (1516). If this dual archaeology[1] lies at the origin of the fluctuations in twentieth-century urbanism, which more or less cedes to the utopia of the ideal city, urbanism more prosaically raises the need to expand cities, to fit them out, to make them more efficient and effective while preventing pollution, encouraging improved hygiene, and putting efficient transport systems in place.

Nowadays, the urbanism that breaks with the traditional division of industrial functionalism (that differentiates the functions of work, accommodation, leisure, and transport, with mobility identified as just one function among many) views mobility as the key determining factor on which all the functions depend. This is hardly surprising, as the European city has been affected by the need for information and communication from the outset: at the diachronic level, we have examples of the inhabited space of the street at the time of the medieval town, the role played by public squares during the Renaissance, the growing importance of urban transport and of public opinion in the industrial era, and the contemporary prevalence of connections (ports, stations, and airports, but also shopping centers, leisure areas, and so on) during the technical revolution now in progress that is making sweeping changes to the relationship with time and space. While the role of mobility is manifest and crucial, it encourages us to imagine territories that make the "passage" from one rhythm to the next possible ... This is the notion behind the concept of the *ville passante* (the flowing city), the city that makes you "pass" from one speed to another. While this expression, coined by the architect David Mangin, must not be confused with that of the pedestrian city, and

1 Françoise Choay, *La Règle et le Modèle: sur la théorie et l'architecture et de l'urbanisme*, the reference book on the links between architecture, utopia, and urbanism.

whereas the *ville passante* values the tangle of territories and connected journeys, it is inseparable from "places" that are not necessarily the monuments that the authorities have for a long time favored but places that render the public aspect of the European city visible. Published in 1908, Émile Magne's *L'Esthétique des villes*[2] reminded readers that every dwelling looks out onto the exterior; that there is no habitation space that is divorced from the urban outdoors that surrounds it. Hence the author's string of evocations of diverse bustling public spaces: the street environment, movement on the roads, processions, markets, bazaars, and fairs, but also cemeteries. There is a long list of these public spaces that urbanism, often reduced to the sole dimension of planning, is tasked with promoting.

## The Imaginary

The European city is complex, all the more so as urbanism is judged by its ability to respect the "movements" of residents who write the account of their cities. There is no city that is not led by an urban imaginary, a fact long demonstrated by *commedia dell'arte*, which saw cities as characters, as so many masked stock characters: Pantalone the merchant is from Venice, Il Dottore—the university-educated doctor—is from Bologna, Arlecchino is from Bergamo, and Pulcinella is from Naples. This is what made Claude Lévi-Strauss say in *Tristes Tropiques* that the city, more particularly the European city that he evokes, is "the human thing par excellence:" "The city situates itself at the confluence of nature and artifice. It is both the object of nature and the subject of culture: individual and group; lived and dreamed; the human thing par excellence." Whereas urbanism materially deploys the urban surroundings likely to enhance urban practices (urban henceforth understood to mean urbanity), these practices are shaped, in part at least, by the body in the sense that each of us writes our city "with our feet;" by a *mise-en-scène*, the illustration of which is the nomadic fairground theater; but also by ritualistic events, collective practices that make the city "the public space" par excellence. It is no coincidence that great cities have their official storytellers who recount their tales, among them Paris and Hugo, Dublin and Joyce, and Lisbon and Pessoa.

2 Émile Magne, *L'Esthétique des villes*, (Gollion: Infolio, 2012).

## The Political Dimension

The complexity of the European city is thus based on a gamble that
remains fully valid, that of associating urbanization and urbanity.
Whereas urbanity is primarily driven by residents' imaginary and
artists' creations, from the outset it has been inseparable from the
political principles that influenced it at the beginning. While the
Greek *polis* and the Roman *urbs* remain references that have lost none
of their force, the European city is genealogically driven by a wish to
distance itself from the feudal hierarchy and to foster the emancipa-
tion of communes. Thus the European city is related to republicanism
and democratic morals. This entails the wish to integrate the immi-
grant: a person arriving from the nearby countryside or from another
land. Such is the cosmopolitan dimension of a European city that
should not forget that its role and its mission are to welcome, to
guarantee arrivals and departures. In this, the city is inextricably
linked to migratory movements, those population displacements
that are to some extent an obstacle and which kindle fear in certain
European countries today. We should remember that the city's
function—in keeping with a tradition that goes back to cities in
the Middle East—is to associate security and hospitality, two values
currently in conflict that constitute the key issue of urban life.
The European city, the one that cannot dissociate identity and cosmo-
politanism, urbanity and urbanization, should not abandon its belief
that hospitality and the ability to ensure collective security ought
to go hand in hand. It is no coincidence that philosophers (Levinas,
Derrida, and others) have revived the theme of the "city of refuge,"
even as urbicide (the destruction of cities during warfare) remains,
as ever, one of the strategies employed by tyrants.

The value of the European city is thus linked to its complexity, in
the sense that its plural history does not involve a utopian model that
has to be applied; in the sense in which it is motivated by a concern
to connect urbanization (which falls within the jurisdiction of urban
plans and projects of every kind) and urbanity (respect for residents
and immigrants) even as urban globalization tends to drive a wedge
between them. Such is the lesson taught by Cerdà, who saw the city
not so much as a story but as a political territory in that it is there that
we share our risks and mutualize our needs. In short, the city is a

miniature welfare state: in this sense, urbanization and urbanity
go hand in hand; they are there to ensure the city does not get carried
away by violence. The European city is not the future of the urban
planet, but its complex archaeology—because it has developed over
the centuries, because it is inextricably linked to a long tradition
of urbanism, the enhancement of the public imaginary, and a political
dimension—is not passé. It has a meaning for cities in Europe
and elsewhere, there where the "squares movement"—Tahrir Square
in Cairo, Maidan Nezalezhnosti (Independence Square) in Kiev—
and the occupied streets in Hong Kong remind us that democratic
energy nourishes the emptiest of our urban spaces, the *agora*, the first
of our public spaces.

**Olivier Mongin.** Philosopher and editor of the review *Esprit*. Among his published works
are *La condition urbaine: La ville a l'heure de la mondialisation* (2005) and *La ville des flux:
L'envers et l'endroit de la mondialisation urbaine* (2013).

# Innsbruck

Austria

**Centrum Odorf**
Froetscher Lichtenwagner
Special Mention 2008

Like many other housing projects, Innsbruck's two Olympic villages were homogeneous residential areas. Although plenty of land was available, the villages had no quality public space, facilities or commercial activity that might intensify their uses. The addition of a multifunctional building surrounding a new square established a new urban center connecting the two villages. At street level, the building houses public facilities and commercial establishments while there are offices and more than a hundred apartments in a seventeen-storied tower at one end. The new complex has brought public facilities to the two Olympic villages and united them by giving them this distinctive, diverse meeting place.

In the past, the Nørrebro area was the scenario for clashes between authorities and demonstrators. It was also a culturally diverse neighborhood that was divided by a wide strip of overgrown land that had become both an eyesore as well as a dangerous vacant site. The objective of Superkilen (or "Super Wedge") was to reclaim this area for public use, while at the same time adopting an approach that celebrated the cosmopolitan local community and rejected the typical gentrification process. Divided into three differentiated parts, the new park features pedestrian and cycling paths, playgrounds and picnic areas as well as objects that recall the residents' home countries.

# Mollet del Vallès
Spain

**Can Mulà Multipurpose Center**
Jordi Cartagena, Enric Serra, Lluís Vives,
Serra-Vives-Cartagena
**Joint Winner 2000**

The demolition of the Can Mulà factory in the 1970s left a large empty space which offered an extraordinary opportunity to rethink the urban center of Mollet. The space was used as a temporary open-air market for some three decades until the municipal government decided to build a multipurpose complex combining its administrative headquarters, apartments, offices, commercial establishments, an underground parking lot, and the municipal market. Thanks to its diversity of uses, types of facilities and the quality of its public spaces, the Can Mulà complex has become a central part of the urban fabric.

# Rotterdam

Netherlands

**Urban Activator**
Atelier Kempe Thill
Special Mention 2010

Located between the Laurenskerk Cathedral and the Delftsevaart Canal, the Grotekerkplein was a dreary, featureless square with no commercial activity. In order to bring it to life and change its backyard appearance, a pavilion-theater was constructed parallel to the watercourse, taking the form of a portico covered by a thirty-meter-long slab framing a stage which is open at the front and back. A sliding curtain of seventy meters in length makes it possible to address audiences on one side of the stage or the other and it can also be used to close off the square in different ways. The space, with its variable appearance, has now become the focus of new cultural activity.

# Espinho

Portugal

**Marinha de Silvade Urban Rehabilitation**

João Paulo Júnior, Carlos A. Sárria, Carlos Alberto Silva

**Special Mention 2002**

railway line, a polluted river and a large canning factory cut off Marinha da Silvade from the rest of ıe town of Espinho. Once a neighborhood of fishermen, Marinha da Silvade was further marginalized the 1980s when the factory, the main source of employment in the area, closed down. At the end the century a general program of urban rehabilitation was approved, this consisting of opening up seafront promenade and new beaches, landscaping the riverbanks, building new bridges, creating reen zones, social housing and providing public facilities. The neighborhood's physical and social arriers were largely removed by this holistic, transversal operation.

# Ljubljana
Slovenia
**Riverside Refurbishment**
Atelier arhitekti, Atelje Vozlič,
BB Arhitekti, Boris Podrecca,
Dans arhitekti, Medprostor,
Trije arhitekti, Urbi
**Joint Winner 2012**

Early in the twentieth century the architect Jože Plečnik transformed Ljubljana into an enlightened city by introducing humanist-inspired public spaces along its riverbanks. A hundred years later, however, the riverside areas had succumbed to the pressure of private cars and there was hardly any space left for pedestrians to enjoy. After 2004, the city hall undertook a diverse series of specific interventions designed to come together in a single large-scale strategy. Footbridges, paths, pavilions, lookouts, docks and parks restored to the river the humanism Plečnik had previously given it. The banks are now wholly accessible to pedestrians and the river is once again the organizing element of an attractive, cultured city.

# Tirana

Albania

**I Like Playing! 100 Playgrounds**
FUSHA
**Finalist 2008**

Over the years, several problems emerged in post-communist Tirana. Large-scale migration and chaotic urban growth with unregulated construction contributed to a deterioration of the city and the public realm. In 2003 the municipality decided to implement a program to recuperate spaces throughout the city to be used for playgrounds and sports areas. One hundred sites were chosen through a citizens' participatory process. Although each project targeted a specific place and limited group of residents, the sum of the interventions represented a significant step towards the recovery of public space in the city.

# Rotterdam

Netherlands

## Westblaak Skatepark

Dirk van Peijpe

Special Mention 2002

Few pedestrians dared to venture onto the central strip of Westblaak Avenue, which was isolated between two lateral roads, each with a lot of traffic. Seeing the need to give this space a new use that would make it dynamic and attractive, the city hall decided to devote it to skateboarders who, frequently arousing ill-feeling because of their intensive use of public space, have problems finding places to gather. Now the central strip of the avenue is well-equipped for skating. Its concave surfaces attract all kinds of wheeled sports enthusiasts as well as onlookers who come to watch their acrobatics. The two groups have transformed the area into a very popular meeting place.

# London
United Kingdom

**Barking Town Square**
Allford Hall Monaghan and Morris,
muf architecture/art
**Joint Winner 2008**

After thoroughgoing transformations in its urban and social fabric, the district of Barking needed a distinguishing space that would rescue its long-lost former identity. Lit by chandeliers and paved in a checkerboard pattern of black and white slabs harking back to the city's Edwardian houses, an arcade was built on the open space in front of the town hall. A new brickwork wall evoking the façades of old industrial buildings joined this construction in an eclectic mix of showy elements to counter the dullness of a place that had lost its attributes. Hence, eccentricity has endowed Barking's new main square with centrality.

Fragments of unused, abandoned or leftover spaces are found on both the peripheries of our cities as well as embedded in the urban fabric. The challenges and opportunities that these spaces offer have been the basis for the design of much of contemporary European public space.

Mar

"Part of our commitment to life entails humanizing our edges and the world's edges, endowing them with some degree of logic and making them intelligible."

# Peripheries

## Francesc Serés

*"The world is a mesh of people with whom we get on well or not so well, and people who get on with the people we get on with. The place that is not reached by the edge of this mesh of people is where the world stops or, if you prefer, it stops being ours."*

Gabriel Ferrater

### Yesterday

For years I hitchhiked from Barcelona to the small town where I grew up. It was the cheapest way to cover the 180 kilometers separating the city from what was then still my home. There were gas stations where you could convince the truckers that you were a nice guy and you'd offer them conversation during the ride. There were rest areas strategically located within the reach of urban bus routes. There were the Mercabarna wholesalers and the loading and unloading areas of the port. Sometimes access was easy, when the subway or a bus left you relatively close. Other times you had to walk, clamber up steep shoulders, cross vacant land, and climb over highway safety barriers.

I've tried to retrace my steps by returning to some of those chaotic routes between industrial estates and highway junctions, but it's impossible. Neither I nor the places are the same. The city has grown with me, building on spaces that didn't belong to it once, more or less as I have had to do with the world, or the part of the world I can call my own. Part of our commitment to life entails humanizing our edges and the world's edges, endowing them with some degree of logic and making them intelligible.

I was twenty years old, with a canvas backpack and a couple of books to ease the waiting or the silence of the journey if the driver didn't want to chat. I'd say I was happy then, or at least I thought I was. Or maybe now I think I was but, the thing is, those roadsides, that vacant unclaimed land gave me everything without asking for anything in return. They were so humble, so neglected, so unloved that they offered me everything the proud city withheld. How can its historic buildings be yours? Yet a highway viaduct gave friendly shade in summer and a solid umbrella on rainy days. All these constructions give so much and ask so little that we don't know the extent to which they save us.

More than twenty years have gone by and, after many journeys, many interviews and photos in industrial estates, many hours of factories and road junctions, and naps in rest areas, I have confirmed that these edges respect me. And I respected the two conditions the periphery set—don't be afraid and don't be contemptuous—without realizing I was doing so.


## Today

Cities try to tell you who they are, looking for differences that make them unique in the eyes of other cities. They emphasize their monumental façades in italics, place their historic neighborhoods in inverted commas, and highlight their main avenues in phosphorescent colors. The fossilized identity of some centers now comes together with the international language of buildings belonging to banks, shopping centers and multinational corporations.

Identity, the real one, this slow-moving chameleon which is constantly changing its colors, shifts to the edge where people can escape the strict norms of the urban condition, where the grip of laws is looser because the price per square meter is less and will not rise again until the edge meets another city.

The error does not lie in quantifying everything. The error is in believing that quantification is constant. Edges don't ask for absolutes. They shift and are modified, very often without any particular plan. Chaos exists, entropy acts, the unforeseen happens, and all three demand a redefinition of the words we have used to characterize the previous edges. The places where I hitchhiked twenty years ago have not disappeared. They are in other places. They have other meanings.

The city is perhaps the most imperfect of the forms of control. We design its mobility, plan its densities, and limit the height of its buildings and speed of its cars. We register its inhabitants and those who can decide about mobility and density. Hitchhiking is forbidden because the self-willed nature of its movements, the simple fact of two strangers traveling together without effective supervision, is scary for the city that is trying to control its periphery.

This is an impossible undertaking. Even if the city installs cameras and photo radar every kilometer and at roundabouts, the edges keep changing. What is the point of putting cameras everywhere when everyone has a cell phone?

## Tomorrow

One of my favorite truck-searching places was the wholesale market of Mercabarna and the factories of Zona Franca. Nowadays, the star of the Llobregat Delta is the new port terminal, which is full of containers. Twenty years ago, all that area was vacant ground and a contaminated river that now seems to be rebelling and trying to civilize the zone. Nature civilizes sometimes.

Nothing defines globalization like its vacant land and containers. Globalization is an immense periphery where everything is possible. Vacant land where everything can be constructed, where there is still space for human decisions, is a local periphery. It is waiting for us to dare to construct where nothing has ever been built, to leave something of ours that defines us. And they ask us if what we construct will be worth the effort.

Containers are a ubiquitous periphery, a standardization of merchandise that lets us relocate factories, which should be in our city, in other cities of faraway countries. Edges are not only physical. Real edges can't be delineated for they have nothing to do with cartography. The network of roads is superimposed on the network of monetary flows, the network of information, the network of airline routes, social networks, and so on.

Faced with the global city, in which capitals, symbols, people and culture are interchangeable, in which spaces, forms, social groups, languages and cultural forms are homogenous, regions, countries and nations are in danger of disappearing. Never mind, there will always be edges; there will always be a periphery to provide a refuge from all-powerful centers. When centers are too strong they end up becoming rigid, sluggish and barren.

When they wanted to grow, modern cities had to bring down walls, escape from the past. Now we need to assault the centers and this can only be done from the edges. Diversity, the capacity for change and even democratic representation all depend on this. Centers tend to uniformity and citizens must resist if they don't want to be swallowed up in the process. Fortunately, edges and peripheries only ask us not to be afraid and not to despise their places or the people who comprise them.

Put like that, it seems easy. It assumes that the center is power and any distancing challenges it. All centers call themselves centers for fear of not being centers. Big city centers, technological and financial centers, powerful but empty, could end up becoming a world that ceases to be ours. It will stop being ours and we shall recover it when, once again, a more powerful center displaces what is displacing us.

Perhaps centers are never wholly ours. The world full of edges is.

**Francesc Serés.** Writer. Author of *La força de la gravetat* (2007) and *La pell de la frontera* (2014).

# Barcelona
Spain

**Environmental Refurbishment of the Besòs River Area**
Barcelona Regional
Special Mention 2002

In the 1960s, channeling work along the last stretch of the Besòs River set up a barrier between the riverside municipalities. Forty years on, thanks to a collaborative effort by administrative branches of different kinds and levels, the riverbed has become a lineal park on the metropolitan scale. Retaining walls incorporate ramps giving access to paths along the banks and the park. The inflatable dams of a pioneering hydraulic system maintain the water level while also acting as lakes which favor a purifying process, thus bringing biological diversity to the river. The new river park is an integrating element, joining adjacent neighborhoods and attracting local residents.

# Zuera

Spain

**Regeneration of the Gállego River and Surroundings**
aldayjover Arquitectura y Paisaje,
Iñaki Alday, Margarita Jover, María Pilar Sancho
**Joint Winner 2002**

The town of Zuera faced away from the Gállego River. Over decades, sedimentation of gravel and dumping of rubble caused rising water levels and more frequent flooding, thus making the riverside area an unstable, marginal place. At the end of the 1990s, the municipality decided to improve the river's hydraulic capacity and the quality of its water, in addition to preventing erosion of its banks, consolidating the urban front, and protecting the natural landscape. A new town park now includes infrastructure, facilities and spaces for a variety of group activities on three large terraces, the lower levels of which are flooded in a seasonal, orderly fashion transforming it into a changing, attractive space that encourages Zuera to face onto its river.

# Zaanstadt
Netherlands

## A8ernA
Pieter Bannenberg, Walter Van Dijk, Kamiel Klaasse,
Mark Linnemann, NL Architects
Joint Winner 2006

Before entering Amsterdam the A8 freeway—built on high concrete pillars—splits the peripheral neighborhood of Koog aan de Zaan into two parts. Once it has crossed the Zaan River,
the viaduct cuts through the main square where, between the town hall and the church, it
interposes a shadowy strip that was once used only as an unofficial parking lot. However, in
2003, this unwelcome barrier was seen as an opportunity to respond to demands expressed
by local residents in a participatory process. It has now been transformed into a large civic
porch joining the two halves of the town and offering a range of facilities including skateboarding parks, games areas, shops, and a jetty.

# Girona

Spain

**Ter River Park**
Joaquim Español, Francesc Hereu
**Special Mention 2000**

When the city of Girona started to grow, the neglected spaces alongside the natural corridor of the Ter River ceased to be marginal. Once susceptible to flooding and used for dumping rubble as well as an illegal construction site, the northern bank has now been transformed into a metropolitan park with fishermen's jetties and bird-watching areas as well as a footbridge connecting it with the city. In the dry season, a dam keeps the water level constant while, when the river rises, an embankment prevents flooding. Thanks to this twofold hydraulic and landscaping intervention, the riverside space is no longer the city's derelict backyard.

# London

United Kingdom

## Opening of Rainham Marshes

Peter Beard_LANDROOM,
Peter Beard, Alexander Gore, Sabba Khan, Dingle Price,
Gregory Ross, Mark Smith, Keita Tajima
**Special Mention 2014**

Rainham Marshes are part of Europe's largest metropolitan area but their rich natural environment and landscape were spared the depredations of urban planning because they were used by the army as a firing range. In 2006 these wetlands were opened to the public and, accordingly, access was improved by means of bridges and footbridges, while platforms were installed for birdwatchers. Rainham Marshes have now entered the collective imaginary of Londoners, who can enjoy an unspoiled landscape within the bounds of the city. Opening the marshes to the public has been essential to ensure their survival by allowing people to discover, enjoy and learn to protect them.

# Begues
Spain

**Vall d'en Joan Landfill Restoration**
Enric Batlle, Joan Roig, Teresa Galí-Izard,
Batlle i Roig Arquitectes
Joint Winner 2004

For three decades, refuse from the metropolitan area of Barcelona was dumped as landfill in a ravine of the Garraf Massif. Pollutants from the site soon leached into aquifers and its methane emissions were equivalent to 20% of the total for the city of Barcelona. When the dump was closed, the artificial topography of terraces and ramps was respected and the ground replanted with local species. Moreover, a biogas plant was installed to produce electricity from the methane. The former landfill site not only contributes in terms of landscaping and energy but it also plays an educational role as it is used to teach schoolchildren about the importance of good waste management.

The relationship between water and the urban fabric is one of the principle identifying characteristics of many European cities. This relationship is complex and changes over time. However, a constant factor is the capacity of the waterfront to continue reinventing its role as the urban façade through a variety of different programs and uses.

Water

front

"The source of the Danube flows through here, Regensburg, Ulm, Dürnstein and Krems flow through here and, a little further on, Budapest will flow by and then Belgrade will flow by, and they'll all end up flowing into the sea."

# Cities Flowing into the Sea

## Adan Kovacsics

One day, a father took his son by the hand and said, "I'm going to take you to Europe. You'll discover the Gothic there."

The son shivered. His feet had trodden the perilous ground of the jungle and he knew the Andes, knew oceans, knew deserts, knew the pyramids, but he'd never seen the Gothic. They lived in Kalandia. The son was a supporter of Kalandia's Blue Phoenix Sports Union, an immigrants' club with famous, awesome forwards, especially Bromson and Sliguvich, who were also immigrants.

Father and son traveled to Europe by boat. This was in the 1960s when people still went from one continent to another by sea. As soon as they disembarked in the first port, they took a train to Vienna, the father's birthplace. He'd then grown up in Budapest and, after the war, had emigrated to Kalandia. In Vienna, he took his son by the hand and they immediately went to see St Stephen's Cathedral, the one with the multihued roof.

"The style that came before the Gothic, the Romanesque, grew out of the crypts and you can always tell that it was born underground. The Gothic, though, strives upwards, seeking the light. That's why it has this penchant for openings and stained glass windows. Every-thing in the Gothic is a complex, mysterious order, like the universe. I refer to the order of numbers. And numbers—as Pythagoras, that wise man of antiquity, suggested—are what link the visible world with the invisible," the father concluded in an enigmatic tone.

They walked around the city center and came to another Gothic church. Standing before the entrance, the father turned around and, gazing into the distance, said, "This church here behind me is called Maria am Gestade, Mary at the Shore. It was given this name because of the river." His black eyes turned sky blue. Cormorants and grebes appeared in them, and a flatboat traveling so slowly that it seemed to be propelled by the arms of exhausted rowers.

The son looked to where his father was looking, but there was no river. There were houses, streets and, in the background, an avenue, but not so much as a single drop of water.

"What river?" he asked.

"The Danube," his father replied.

That, then, was the first time the son saw the Danube. In the form of an absence.

"One of the branches of the Danube used to run through here," the father said. "That's why this church has such a strange form. One part of the central nave is narrower than the rest. The Gothic is all perfect lines and exaltation of numbers, but they couldn't stick to the rules in Maria am Gestade because of the river. Yes, one of the branches of the river flowed through here but then they diverted it away. They regulated it. In the nineteenth century," the father said and suddenly fell silent, as if he'd bitten off too much to chew. "In the nineteenth century," he continued after a pause, "they demolished the city walls and regulated the course of the river. The city had to be protected from floods and they needed land for building houses. They carried out large-scale construction work. Regulate, channel, construct— the entire second half of the nineteenth century is concentrated in these verbs. In this city," he went on, "the Vienna Danube Regulation commission was established in the middle of the century, in 1850, and its job was to regulate the river. It held a meeting that lasted twenty years. One member of the commission nodded off with his finger stuck at some point on the map of the city unfolded on the table. He woke up gray at the temples. He'd spent several years dreaming about the Danube. They studied a number of possible diversions, the most favorable being the one that was closest to the city. Yet they discarded it, among other reasons, to conserve the recreational zone, the Prater. The majority of the commission's members voted for diverting the river away from the city center because, anyway, they said, 'it's inclined to go to the left,' by which they meant it tended to flow northeastwards, frequently flooding large areas of land. The city hasn't forgotten that commission. One of the streets in Vienna is named after its president, Florian von Pasetti ..."

The next day, father and son left for Budapest. At the border they were afraid. The watchtowers, the methodical checks in the compartment of their passenger car, the soldiers lined up on both sides of the train, the minutes that went by without the train moving weren't meant to inspire serenity. Once in the capital, they stayed with relatives who lived in a very small flat, which they shared with another family named Szabó. They shared the kitchen, they shared the bathroom, and they bumped into each other in the passageway, holding their soap and towel. "You go first." "No, you go …" The atmosphere was oppressive. They were alert to the slightest sound. They spoke in whispers. "Don't go into the kitchen now. One of the Szabós has just gone in," they'd murmur.

Asphyxiated by the atmosphere in his relatives' home, the father took his son out for walks. He led him to the bank of the Danube because his relatives lived nearby, in District 13. They walked along Pozsonyi út.

"You know, the riverbank used to be here before they regulated the river, right where this street is," the father told the son. "And, for example, the land where the parliament building now stands was part of the riverbed two hundred years ago. There were a lot of very big floods. In the second half of the nineteenth century, one of the main concerns was to protect the city against flooding. The first measure was building big dikes. They constructed wharves and dredged the Danube. In the neighborhood now known as Lágymányos, it went from being one kilometer wide to less than four hundred meters. Narrowing it and straightening it was an important step. Remember this, my son, because what was good for Vienna was good for Budapest too: regulate, channel, construct …"

Father and son sat down on the quay near the parliament and stared at the river. It was a mighty river, yet it flowed sedately by. It was springtime.

"Contemplations, that's what all beings are." The father blurted this out, without looking up from the water. "And one sees the river flowing by. In Vienna they moved the river away, because they didn't want to see anything flowing by. The source of the Danube flows through here, Regensburg, Ulm, Dürnstein and Krems flow through here and, a little further on, Budapest will flow by and then Belgrade will flow by, and they'll all end up flowing into the sea."

Then the father started talking about bridges. Every time he mentioned them, his black eyes lit up, taking on a golden gleam because of the kinship between gold and darkness.

"What you see there," he said, pointing left, "is the Lánchíd, the Chain Bridge, the first permanent bridge to be constructed between Buda and Pest. Before that, around the turn of the eighteenth and nineteenth centuries, there was another one that they used to take down in winter. The bridges were destroyed in the Second World War and reconstructed afterwards," he continued. When he spoke of the war, he struggled for air. He started to cough. Between coughs, he told the son how the Germans blew up all the bridges when, with the Red Army advancing, they retreated from Pest and took up a fortified position in Buda. Huge chunks of stone and metal were left lying in the river.

Father and son returned to Kalandia. By sea—the way things had to be done. Shortly after that trip, the father died. He suddenly felt as if he couldn't breathe. He was in his shed and there was no air in the shed. He went out into the garden and there was no air in the garden either. By the time they got him to the hospital, it was too late.

Decades later and now an adult, the son read a book in which Budapest appeared as did, conspicuously, the Danube. Yes, that's where the Hungarian Nazis took the Jews during the war. They led them down to the wharf, shot them and threw them into the river. The book describes it thus: "Supreme hostility appeared, the kind that simply wanted your life, and if you didn't offer an alternative solution, it was ready to shoot you and throw you into the Danube to be swept away by the current … The people who were taken to the bank of the Danube had to stand in a row facing the river. Then there was a volley from behind."

One day, the son went back to Budapest. He returned to the quay where he used to go with his father when they felt oppressed by their relatives' flat, the home of whispers. There was now a monument in this place, a line of shoes. Sixty pairs of metal shoes spread over some forty meters along the bank of the Danube, in memory of the Hungarian Jews murdered by the members of the Arrow Cross Party in 1944 and 1945. Exactly the same place where he and his father had sat to contemplate the river!

For the second time, the son saw the Danube in the form of an absence.

**Adan Kovacsics.** Writer and translator of Hungarian and Austrian literature into Spanish. Author of *Guerra y lenguaje* (2007).

# Oslo
Norway
**Norwegian National Opera**
Snøhetta
Joint Winner 2010

During the twentieth century the infrastructure for the Oslo port eventually surrounded the old center of Bjørvika, thus condemning it to become an isolated and neglected zone. At the turn of the new century, the Norwegian government decided to transform Bjørvika into a representative neighborhood that would articulate Oslo's relationship with its fjord. The first step in the process was to construct a great opera house on one of the wharves. Visitors now have access to the waterfront and, moreover, can walk up the gently sloping roof of the new building to higher points from which they can enjoy fine views over the fjord.

# Marseille

France

**Vieux Port Renovation**
Michel Desvigne Paysagiste MDP, Foster + Partners,
Tangram, INGEROP, AIK
**Joint Winner 2014**

Despite its central location and the beauty of its setting, the old port of Marseilles had fallen into a state of neglect and disrepair at the end of the twentieth century. Cluttering the zone with architectural and visual barriers, yacht clubs deprived the public of access to 80% of the wharves. Priority given to cars further discouraged pedestrians. Although the reforms undertaken in 2009 by the municipality still permit the presence of leisure craft, which encourage economic and group activity, they also give full access to all citizens. While other city ports combat economic decline by privatizing and thereby excluding the public, the Vieux Port redevelopment has extended its condition of a shared space open to everyone.

# Benidorm
Spain

**Western Beach Promenade**
Office of Architecture in Barcelona,
Carlos Ferrater, Xavier Martí Galí
Special Mention 2010

Renovation work on the Western Beach walkway in the 1970s left it with nondescript paving and a concrete balustrade which obstructed views of the sea and only gave access to the sand at two-hundred-meter intervals. A redevelopment in 2009 notably improved Benidorm's relationship with the sea. The new promenade consists of a succession of concave and convex walls delimiting terraces paved in different colors and giving better access to the beach with ramps and steps. The bright, sinuous forms embrace the heterogeneous skyscrapers which compete to take over the coast, bringing them into a single unitary scheme.

As the port neighborhood of Islands Brygge industrialized and then fell into disuse in the second half of the twentieth century, the waters of the canal passing through it became so polluted that the busy Rysensteen public baths had to be closed. In 2003, when the old factories were replaced by residential buildings, a waterfront park was opened together with the Harbor Bath, a floating wooden platform with four swimming pools. Its clean, safe water has restored to the neighborhood the popularity it enjoyed in its Rysensteen heyday, while diving boards and handrails evoke the old industrial landscape.

# Zadar
Croatia
**Sea Organ**
Nikola Bašic
Joint Winner 2006

The western shoreline of the Zadar Peninsula had not recovered from bombing attacks during World War II and despite its superb sunsets, remained a run-down, rarely visited space. However, when tourists started coming to Croatia it was necessary to construct a wharf for cruise ships and a waterfront walk leading to the city. With this new construction, land and sea were united by a set of steps where people can sit and gaze at the horizon and, apart from visual pleasures, the steps also conceal tubes which make musical sounds with the movement of the waves, like a huge sea organ.

In the contemporary European city, productivity and economic vitality are generated not only in the markets themselves, but also in other types of public spaces that have been recuperated for a variety of activities and events.

Market

"If you want to keep the markets informal and open, you must have pretty strong government policies against global capitalism."

# Interview

## Richard Sennett
### in conversation with David Bravo

**DB:** Today in Europe factories are closing everywhere. At the same time, the markets are becoming bigger and bigger with financial control in the hands of just a few. How can people make their living under these conditions?

**RS:** What I'm familiar with is a certain kind of market, the "informal market," rather than shopping malls or markets of a more upscale kind. Economically speaking, by "informal market" we mean a market in which there's no fixed price for goods and people have to interact, like in a souk. In the developing world, in places like Delhi or Medellín, these informal markets are places where very poor people get a chance to participate in the economy by doing something other than manufacturing.

These markets are often semilegal and deal in goods that have "fallen off the back of a truck," but they're also entry points for poor people into the economy of the cities: you find them all over the developing world. And what makes them entry points is economic informality, which as I've just said, means that the price of goods is never fixed.

What's happened in the case of globalized markets is that they've removed informality. With globalized goods, the small informal market is always at a disadvantage because the only people who can engage in discounting are large firms, which tend to be exclusive.

I did a study in the 1980s of a market for the working-class population on 14th Street in New York, a big, wide street where all the subway lines converge. This was the city's working-class public space, the space where people sold everything—from cameras, to underwear, to food—on overturned cartons out on the street and in abandoned factories they'd colonized. It was semilegal, the mafia was partially involved, but it was for immigrants, and at that point in New York it was a lifeline because the city's industries were shrinking, and this was the kind of activity they could get involved in.

So in my view, the difference between the shopping mall and the open-air market is who can engage in economics there. And when you start thinking in terms of social class, the nature of the space becomes entirely different: the space has to be informalized to allow people to enter; the entry points are the streets, street corners, and disused spaces formerly serving other purposes.

As a practical matter, I'm interested in how to informalize spaces in the city so that poor people won't find it so hard to become part of it. And in this context I'm particularly concerned with how the United States tends to use planning laws and planning regulations to get rid of informality.

**DB: What are the features, or the shape, that a market should have in order to be open and democratic?**

**RS:** It shouldn't have a shape, that's the whole point. It should take many shapes depending on where it is. It should be a place people can colonize, otherwise it becomes an architectural statement. And once you've made an architectural statement, you disempower people who can't afford to work in it.

Borough Market is a very good example of this because it's no longer for the people who were originally there. Borough Market is for the haute bourgeoisie, it's very expensive. Basically, what was destroyed was a market not just for poor people but also for lower middle-class people in south London: the prices went up and up, and more and more small traders were eliminated.

Most of the traders at Borough Market are representatives of large firms; it's become gentrified. I don't believe in architectural form if what you're interested in is economic participation in a city. I don't think the fact that it's an open-air covered porch like Borough Market is going to get you there. This is capitalism we're talking about, not architecture.

**DB: The market forms part of the city's DNA. How can we avoid gentrification like in Borough Market? How can we let small traders and poor people participate in this space?**

**RS:** This is a very practical issue. But what we've decided in London, and in New York too, I think, is that one aspect of this is to create alternative spaces.

In New York, the government intervenes to stop certain forms of commercial gentrification. I'll give you a very concrete example of this: a shop in New York that has been trading at a certain level for thirty years gets a new landlord who says "I'm going to charge you five times more rent." And you say "Five times more? You can't do that! I can make a profit with a reasonable rent increase but I can't pay you five times more." So the landlord says "goodbye, then."

What we're trying to do is prevent this by creating the same kind of rent control for certain small businesses as the one that's applied to housing. This is one way to slow gentrification down.

For most people, the example of London's Borough Market is a loathsome one because it's now a popular place for well-to-do ladies and gentlemen to have lunch. So the alternative is places like Leather Lane, which is an open-air market, near me, where there are only small businesspeople. In other words, you can't be a representative of a big firm wearing a peasant's hat to look like what you're not, because only the small shopkeepers and merchants can trade there.

What's important about this is that if the free market operated without government interference, these people would be gone. It's kind of ironic that in order to keep a market open, you need lots of government interference as a counterbalance to the normal economic forces, and this here in Britain, which is now a nation of financiers, people who have been seduced by finance.

So, on the one hand, they see that the small high-street shops and traditional small markets are being destroyed by big firms or by expensive gentrification projects. And on the other, they're convinced that the government shouldn't interfere with the market. But you can't have it both ways. If you want to keep the markets informal and open, you must have pretty strong government policies against global capitalism.

**DB: Let's talk about factories that stimulated production and the influx of people into European cities during the twentieth century. What we have now are vacant plants with the companies going to China and other parts of the developing world. What can we do?**

RS: This is another issue, but I don't think it's economically feasible for all the people who used to be employed as semiskilled or skilled labor in factories to become entrepreneurs. I mean, one of the fantasies of finance capitalism is that everybody should become small-scale entre-preneurs with small-scale businesses, a very self-serving fantasy: "Be like me, I make a million a year, so you can too," you know, "be entrepreneurial," and so on. And for a while people bought that; but it's a fantasy, there's not enough room, there's not enough need for it.

What we should do is develop new sites for skilled production, which is what I argued for in my book *The Craftsman*. But again, you need government support. If a company is tempted to go overseas for unskilled labor, the government should invest in building up enter-prises that require skilled labor and train the workers for them.

An example of this in Britain is the wind farm. The mechanism for the wind farm—the propellers—was invented about 200 yards from where I live in London, but it's manufactured in Vietnam. The British government did nothing: "After all, how could we interfere with the market?" So even though the idea originated here, all those jobs went there. Now it's being produced in Vietnam, it's hugely profit-able, and the Vietnamese are putting their money back into training formerly unskilled workers so that they can take over more and more of the fabrication process. The British government's response continues to be "Oh please, interfere with the market? How could we do that?"

It's a kind of paradigm of the notion that I think advanced capitalist societies have, which is to let the productive process go elsewhere: "We'll do the nonproductive thing by making everybody a web designer." And the result is that we are losing more and more employ-ment and not building a skilled labor base. So, in my opinion, the answer to the absence of production is new kinds of production, not more markets.

Isn't it amazing that this capitalist ideology is so deeply rooted in us? The reason why people are still reeling from the 2008 financial recession is that the government was spending too much money, hence the IMF reproach to Greece: "Oh, you retire too early; you must repay your debts!" And despite the fact that the IMF forgave debts, this is what they technically call a haircut for forty-six other countries. It's due to this mentality that the financial markets are primary and the financiers must be paid back: they can't make a loss, they're too big to fail. So you take the money out of welfare projects, social investments and so on.

There's been a process of gentrification driven by different kinds of financing that tends to favor central spaces, regenerated places, and push the poor out into marginal areas. This used to be true only in Latin America and Asia, but over the last twenty years it's become true in Europe as well.

I'll tell you a story: my son is a sculptor, and for fifteen years he had his studio under one of the railway arches in Hoxton, a trendy neighborhood in London. Last year he got a notification from the owner, namely the city of London, saying "We cannot renew your lease because we have a potential tenant for your premises who is willing to pay six times what you are paying." He was furious about this because all around him what's there now are fashion designers. And he said to the person who was displacing him, "Where do you think I should go now? The city owns lots of properties." And he answered, "Get as far away from the center as you can." So in Hoxton, a deep gentrification process is under way.

This interview took place at the London School of Economics, August 5, 2015.

**Richard Sennett.** Sociologist. Professor of Sociology at the London School of Economics and Professor of Humanities at New York University. Author of the trilogy *The Craftsman* (2008), *Together: The Rituals, Pleasures and Politics of Cooperation* (2012), and *The Open City* (2016).

**David Bravo.** Architect. Editor of www.publicspace.org

# Celje
Slovenia

**New Market**
Ark Arhitektura Krušec, Lena Krušec,
Tomaž Krušec, Vid Kurinčič
Selected 2010

Traditionally the market in Celje was a vibrant hub in the heart of the town. However, the old, mid-twentieth-century building had fallen into an appalling state of disrepair. In 2006 the municipality decided to build a new market on the same site, and this project was undertaken as an opportunity to redevelop and regenerate the entire area. The market was designed as a contemporary reinterpretation of the typical town market, with a huge roof covering a public square and an open perimeter that establishes a direct relationship with the four adjacent streets.

# Ghent

Belgium

## Stadshal

Robbrecht en Daem architecten,
Marie-José van Hee architecten
Finalist 2014

The demolition of a block of houses between the cathedral and the city hall obliterated the typically medieval density of the old center of Ghent. The three small squares surrounding the space spread into a single, oversized and excessively homogenous esplanade, much of which was used as an open-air parking lot. Half a century later, a large public porch has restored the space's former volume and reestablished the lost dimensions of the three squares. Its two steeply sloping pitched roofs, which fit in well with the surrounding Gothic buildings without attempting to replicate them, provide shelter for a variety of public uses, including the weekly market.

# Figueres
Spain
**Photovoltaic Cover**
Cáceres Arquitectes, Rafael de Cáceres, Xavier de Cáceres
Finalist 2012

With the intention of refurbishing Plaça de Catalunya in the center of Figueres, a huge urban cover has been installed that functions as a place that is both protected from the elements as well as open to the city around it. Its innovative photovoltaic system saves on materials and energy and the diffused light as well as transversal ventilation that cools the interior are reminiscent of the traditional Mediterranean markets. A versatile and multifunctional space, the structure takes on the role of a civic center that provides the scenario for the weekly market, fairs, concerts, and other events.

'or more than a century, the Beşiktaş market has enlivened the surrounding streets from its trian-
;ular-shaped crossroads position in a zone full of crowded restaurants. In recent years, however,
leterioration of the structure and its questionable health standards made it difficult for fish sellers
:o compete with shopping malls on the outskirts of the city. These may be cleaner but they are also
nuch less sustainable and beneficial in terms of the quality of urban life. The market has now been
:otally overhauled and, although its roof and installations have been replaced, it has retained its former
:ondition of an open porch blending in well with everyday life in the surrounding neighborhoods.

# Cangas do Morrazo
Spain

**Fishermen's Huts**
Irisarri + Piñera
Special Mention 2010

The considerable nautical and fishing activity in the port of Cangas does not detract from the beauty of the bay in which it is set. Yet, despite its splendid views of the sea and town, the breakwater was used as the yacht club parking lot rather than as a place where people could walk. It was only frequented by anglers who fished from the rocks. When it was transformed into a seaside promenade, forty huts were built where fishermen could store their tackle. Walkers can now enjoy the views as well as being able to observe the tasks of a productive activity that has a long history in Cangas.

# Ripoll
Spain

**La Lira Theatre**
RCR Aranda Pigem Vilalta Arquitectes, Joan Puigcorbé
**Special Mention 2014**

A vacant lot with blind flank walls on either side broke the continuity of Ripoll's riverfront façade, leaving an unsightly gap where town and river met. Yet the Ter River was an important part of the town as it had supplied water for its famous forges ever since the Middle Ages. A large porch now shelters an open, versatile space which is ideal for fairs and markets, not least because a new foot-bridge crossing the river has made it a busy gateway to the old town center. Both porch and bridge are constructed with weathering steel, which blends well with the aged façades of the adjacent buildings as well as fittingly evoking the town's metallurgical tradition.

# Leipzig
Germany
**Lene Voigt Park**
Gabriele G. Kiefer, Büro Kiefer
Joint Winner 2002

The neighborhood of Reudnitz was hit by unemployment and had very little local business. Moreover, for decades after a bombing attack on the railroad station during World War II, it had been split apart by the resulting stretch of disused land. After years of mobilization, the site was transformed into a public park in a process during which citizens were involved in planning the project, the construction of some of its parts, and its subsequent management. Instead of using gardens as an ornamental feature, the park has combined vegetable plots cultivated by local residents with vestiges of the old railroad track, thus evoking the site's productive past.

Increasingly, European public space is being generated from the bottom-up. Citizens are engaging in participative projects that transform underutilized urban spaces into places that provide services and amenities for their respective neighborhoods and communities.

Demo

"The personal experience in public, acting together with others, inventing new forms of interaction and mutual recognition, has a transformative effect on both individuals and society."

# Urban Space for Performative Citizenship
## For a Creative and Grounded Politics

# Nilüfer Göle

New forms of public performative politics bring city and citizens
to the core of democratic agendas. A new script for democracy is
drafted and the authors of this screenplay are not exclusively from
western society, since it is written not only in Latin alphabet but
also in Arab calligraphy, from the East and elsewhere. There is no
single hub in which the agenda for the emancipatory potential of
city and cities is set. Democratic scenarios are played out in different cities, in different public places from Tahrir Square in Cairo
to Maidan Nezalezhnosti (Independence Square) in Kiev, from Gezi
Park in Istanbul to the indignados at the Puerta del Sol in Madrid,
from Occupy Wall Street in New York to the Hydrangea Revolution
in Tokyo. Citizens facing risks and threats of all kinds, ecological
or economic, living under different political regimes, liberal or
despotic, are inspired by each other's upheaval and protest symbols
and produce a chain of alliances with shared democratic aspirations.
In Tokyo Hydrangea activists are inspired by the Jasmine Revolution
in Tunisia, while Gezi Park activists resonate and enter into
solidarity with their Puerta del Sol and Zuccotti Park counterparts.
Globalization is a process that permeates our lives in many insidious
ways; it circulates without human faces, captured as neoliberalism,
and renders the sphere of politics ineffective. The public assemblies
bring the polis to the forestage and open up the arena of politics to
citizens, to criticisms of the "colonization of everyday life" practices,
and defy the neoliberal democratic frames.

Citizens acting together and enacting in public, collectively manifesting their presence, are resetting democratic agendas. Citizens from all over the world are disputing their right for alternative forms of society making. In public, they manifest their presence and experience each other's difference without trying to supersede it in a form of collective identity, whether defined in national and ethnic, or majority and minority terms. They appropriate a new/old space for politics threatened by authoritarianism, neoliberalism or terrorism. The traditional public square or *maidan* becomes the hub of urban democratic imaginaries as actors from different horizons and an entire array of groups occupy it and turn it into a sort of theatrical scene. The domain of showing and communication, the visual arts and the social media are becoming an integral part of democratic enactment. Public space democracy emerges in its own political terms, in distinction from avenues of parties and voting. Occupy movements are not conducted by enduring political organizations or represented by leaders. They appear, make citizens appear and set an example of horizontal engagement with fellow citizens. They disappear and retreat from the public square but their impact seems to persist. One speaks of the Arab Spring, the Gezi Spirit in Turkey or the 15-M climate in Spain. The notions of "spring, spirit and climate" refer to an opening of a window of opportunity, a microclimate, a pacified atmosphere and a civic attitude generated by these collective experiences. They cannot be captured in well-defined structures, but the political "style" remains pervasive and diffuse by nature. They are outside the avenues of power and representative politics; however, they provide a new grammar, set a new horizon for politics. In Madrid and in Barcelona the two women mayors were carried to power by the 15-M climate. And in Turkey the Gezi Spirit had an impact in setting the agenda during the 2015 general elections. The Gezi-inspired Kurdish opposition party adopted a politics of coexistence among all minorities, religious and ethnic, including a homosexual candidate on its list. The adoption of humor in the communication style contributed to tempering the polarized, tense political atmosphere and created a microclimate. The civil societal "vote and beyond" initiative that emerged after the Gezi protests surveyed the ballots and ensured that the elections were held without fraud. The elections put a brake on the threat of authoritarianism, the tyranny of the majority and the mega political and development projects in Turkey. The Deleuzian politics of *mineur* seemed to make a major difference.

The personal experience in public, acting together with others, inventing new forms of interaction and mutual recognition, has a transformative effect on both individuals and society. Mostly they become the "actor" in action, while performing in public in each other's presence. They explore new forms of linking the personal to the public agency. The copresence in the public square of different citizens and their enactment of alternative forms of being and living together characterize these movements. They bear some features in common with the '68 countercultural movements, namely the festive and communal character. The active presence of women, migrant, ethnic and sexual minorities (LGBTQ individuals), soccer fans and the users of social media give a playful and heterogeneous outlook to these gatherings defying the masculine conceptions of power and citizenship. The "hactivists," who are among the actors, play an important role as they ensure the flow of communication between activists, create secure virtual spaces and thereby avoid the obstruction and manipulation of information by governments.

The public gatherings are played out in the center of the city. Despite violent police intervention, ordinary citizens do not hesitate to take to the streets and block avenues, neighborhoods, and their cities' central spaces. They are distinct from social movements, are not labeled according to the nature of the crowd, class origin, ethnic identity, or any sociological category, but named after the places they appropriate, occupy, and inhabit, such as Tahrir Square, Gezi Park, Wall Street, and so on. They reach out from the public square to the streets, to the crowd, from the capital cities to little towns.

The restoration of the autonomy of the public sphere is at the heart of these gatherings. In some places, the public sphere is regulated by the disciplinary powers of the State, imposing religious or secular codes of behavior and monitoring lifestyles. In many other places the public space risks being confiscated by private capital seeking real-estate rents and debt-fueled consumerism. Gezi Park mobilized young inhabitants in Istanbul defending a "few trees" against the urban plan to construct a shopping mall. Beyond ecological sensibility, it aroused new critical consciousness for the defense of an accessible public space open to inhabitants.

As David Harvey argues: "The creation of a new urban commons, a public sphere of active democratic participation, requires that we roll back that huge wave of privatization that has been the mantra of a destructive neoliberalism." The "right to the city," he writes, is "not merely a right of access to what the property speculators and state planners define, but an active right to make the city different, to shape it more in accord with our heart's desire, and to remake ourselves thereby in a different image."[1] There is a place for imagination and desire that play their part in changing ourselves and changing our world. A dialectical relation lies at the heart of human action. All of us, he argues, are architects of a sort. As the architect erects a structure in the imagination before materializing it upon the ground, we individually and collectively make the city through our daily actions, engagements and desires.

The square becomes the stage where actors improvise and perform. In the square they create libraries, organize workshops, dance, compose music or distribute food. They rehearse together new forms of citizenship. The square presents an opportunity and space for congregation, debate, support and reassembling but also for exploration and creativity. The performative and visual repertoire of action staged in a given physical locality opens the way for new forms of public agency and brings the cultural-artistic realm to the fore.

The place is not an empty neutral place as Henri Lefebvre argued. It is not devoid of power relations or disputes over its ownership. It is also deeply imbued with layers of social and architectural memory. The public space offers a scene for present-day politics, but also an historical archive with different temporalities, inhabitants, monuments and events. Present-day disputes over the usage and ownership of the space bring different epochal layers and their competing interpretations to the surface. Politics of city memory become part of global democratic agendas. Historical effacement of some forms of heritage and marketing of others become decisive in signifying the past. The Gezi site in Istanbul exemplified the

1 David Harvey, "The Right to the City," in *International Journal of Urban and Regional Research*, vol. 27.4 (December 2003), 939–941.

dispute over the city's history. Construction of a shopping mall and luxury apartments, rebuilding the Ottoman military barracks to signify the Ottoman past, and remembering the presence of an old Armenian cemetery and hospital all collided together.

The public virtues of common life, peaceful coexistence, mutual respect and civility become paramount for democracy. The peace of everyday life is threatened by the pace of neoliberalism, as well as by fear of terrorism. The uses of hate discourse and violence in public life remain a major concern for democracies. Multicultural migrant societies bring different cultural codes foreign to each other into closer proximity without providing a framework for intercultural communication and living together.

The serial terrorist killings perpetrated by the jihadists in January 2015 in several European capital cities shook the very foundations of everyday public life. *Charlie Hebdo* cartoonists in their workplace were shot dead, while Jews shopping in their kosher supermarket were taken hostage in Paris or assaulted while praying in a synagogue in Denmark.

To condemn the increasing violence and stand in solidarity with Jews in Europe, more than one thousand Muslims joined hands and formed a human shield around Oslo's synagogue, offering symbolic protection for the city's Jewish community. Chanting "No to anti-Semitism, no to Islamophobia," Norway's Muslims formed what they called a ring of peace. They offered us an opportunity to rethink politics from the perspective of performative citizenship, protecting the everyday life practices of their fellow citizens and enacting co-citizenship between Muslims and Jews in Europe.

**Nilüfer Göle.** Sociologist. Director of Studies at the École des Hautes Études en Sciences Sociales in Paris. Author of *Musulmans au quotidien: Une enquête européenne sur les controverses autour de l'islam* (2015).

# Berlin
Germany
**Volkspalast**
ZwischenPalast-Nutzung,
Volkspalast Philipp Oswalt
**Special Prize of the Jury 2006**

The parliament of the German Democratic Republic was constructed over the foundations of the Berliner Stadtschloss, a baroque palace which was demolished in 1950 by the GDR authorities, who deemed it to be a symbol of Prussian imperialism. After the Berlin Wall came down, asbestos fiber was detected and the building was dismantled, leaving only the basic structure. In 2003, the Bundestag decided to complete the demolition of what it saw as a vestige of totalitarianism and, literally, to reconstruct the old palace. However, in the three years before it disappeared, a citizens' movement turned the skeleton of the building into a temporary experimental cultural center, thus demonstrating that changing the use and sense of a traumatic place is better than destroying it.

# Paris

France

**Passage 56**

atelier d'architecture autogérée

Special Mention 2010

Rue Saint Blaise runs through the 20th *arrondissement* of Paris, a district notable for its density,
cultural diversity and absence of good public space. At number 56 on this street an empty strip of
land, the by-product of a badly designed housing block dating from the 1980s, fell into disuse and
neglect and was closed off with bars. In an unusual initiative of cooperation between the public
administration, local businesses and neighborhood associations, a participative process transformed
the space into a collectively-managed vegetable garden where local residents hold workshops on
ecological horticulture as well as gastronomic events featuring food from all around the world.

# Madrid
Spain
**Occupation of the
Puerta del Sol**
Special Category 2012

On May 15, 2011, with the Arab Spring as background, and in a context of serious economic crisis and disrepute of public institutions, citizens demonstrated in more than fifty Spanish cities to call for a better democratic system. In Madrid, the protest ended with a spontaneous camp being set up in a central square, the Puerta del Sol. A mix of improvised shelters and commercial brands of tents, with special shared spaces for libraries and day nurseries, it sometimes took on the dense morphology of a casbah while, on other occasions, it opened out to make space for new demonstrations. Dismantled after a few weeks, this evanescent city bears witness to the basic role played by public space in democracies.

# Bucharest

Romania

**Public Swimming Pool**
studioBasar
Finalist 2014

As happens elsewhere in the old center of Bucharest, cars, whether parked or moving, normally occupy most of the surface of Arthur Verona Street. In the summer of 2012, the residents on this street decided to clear it of vehicles for three days and install a temporary swimming pool made of hired pallets and plastic sheeting. Despite its fleeting existence, this successful experiment reinforced the street's social, cultural and political dimensions by giving them priority over its normal roadway function. Moreover, the participants will never forget the abiding lesson that a more just and sustainable way of being in the street is possible.

Fed up with being banished from the few places where it was possible to skateboard in the town of Arbúcies, a group of adolescents between eleven and eighteen years organized in order to demand their own skateboarding space. They sought advice from a team of architects specializing in the construction of skateboard parks from recycled materials and found an ideal site near a sports complex. After rigorously working on the project together, and managing to obtain permission from the municipality of Arbúcies to construct the park themselves, they eventually produced a skating zone which has also become a very popular meeting place.

# Turin

Italy

**Barca Workshop**
raumlaborberlin
Selected 2014

Located on the periphery of Turin, the Barca neighborhood is a typical example of housing developed
in the 1960s and 1970s with few amenities or public installations for the residents. The objective o
the workshops conducted as part of *Cantiere Barca* has been to involve young people in a series o
projects that improve their neighborhood. Using recycled materials and by working together, the
participants have constructed elements and places that enhance public life. At the same time they
are empowered to become active citizens engaged in their community.

Numerous fountains are to be found throughout the historic city of Guimarães. But, as in most places, they are objects to be observed rather than to be interacted with, even during the hottest months. This series of interventions invited people to rethink the role of fountains in the cityscape by transforming them into public pools. Utilizing elements such as plastic tables and chairs, colorful balls, inflatable water toys, and standard pool stairs, this low-cost proposal provided spontaneous and joyful relief from the summer heat for both residents and tourists alike.

# Magdeburg
Germany
**Open-Air Library**
KARO*, Architektur+ Netzwerk
Joint Winner 2010

As in many other East German towns, the postindustrial cityscape in the neighborhood of Salbke featured many closed businesses and derelict factories. A large part of the population was unemployed. In this setting of physical and social depression a vacant lot, earmarked years earlier for a public library, remained unoccupied. Tired of the municipal authorities' inaction, the local residents worked on a realistic plan and produced a real-scale model made of beer crates, constructed *in situ*. The end result was an open-air library stocked with books they had collected and managed by the citizens.

...and the library was officially opened

REFLE

# CTIONS

**FROM EUROPE AND BEYOND**

*"There is a European-wide consensus that public space contributes to the common good, and that quality of the public space can and does make a difference."*

# Middle Ground

## Hans Ibelings

.

One of the books I would love to write, but probably never will, is a history of the European exterior, a complement to Mario Praz's inspiring 1963 monograph on the European interior, *La filosofia dell'arredamento*. Praz covers interiors from Greek and Roman Antiquity up to English Arts & Crafts and Art Nouveau, mainly through paintings, watercolors and engravings. These images reflect the domestic bliss of an elite who could afford this happiness and afford to commission artists to depict it. Despite the double layer of mediation—this being Praz's reading of images that by themselves offer a filtered interpretation of an idealized, protected daily life in the interiors of a privileged class—the book manages to transmit the sense of a bygone life between walls.

In the hands of a writer as perceptive and talented as Praz, a book on the exterior world would be able to revive the fleeting past life of streets and squares. Just as many interiors are taken for granted, so is the bread-and-butter of the city, the streets and squares which are crucial to keep it going. They are so ubiquitous that they mostly lead an inconspicuous and unnoticed life as thoroughfares and intersections.

Praz restricted himself to Europe (with the exception of one single image of an interior in New York), and there are good reasons to limit this hypothetical book on public space to Europe as well. Obviously, neither private interiors nor public outdoor spaces are exclusively European. There are interiors in every building, and public spaces in every village, town and city on every continent. Yet despite their global presence, public spaces elsewhere do not necessarily have the same significance as in Europe. While Europe cannot claim ownership or parenthood of public space in general, it seems that there is something very European about the way the publicness of its public spaces is understood. And I am saying this with full realization of the danger of sounding Eurocentric and awareness of the difficulty of truly understanding what this publicness entails and encompasses. After all, many of the spaces that are public in the legal sense—meaning they are universally accessible—are not public when social interaction is taken as a defining criterion. Not everything with paint on it is a painting, and accessibility alone does not make a space public.

**Occupation of the Puerta del Sol**
Madrid, 2012

**Place au Changement**
Collectif Etc
Saint-Étienne, 2012

Public spaces include everything from the ceremonial to the mundane. The far ends of the total field covered by public space are relatively easy to identify, and are common nearly everywhere. One end consists of ceremonial public spaces, which are intended to be exactly that. Usually they are large and designed to be monumental. The typical example is the main central square, often in front of one of the seats of power or another important public building. These official places are the sites of celebration of mass gatherings and the symbolic representation of imposing abstractions such as state, power, religion, citizenship or nationality. They are the common sites for demonstrations of and sometimes against power. Their size allows for parades, festivals, protests, concerts and all kinds of Potemkin-like events which gather large numbers of people but mask the absence of a truly public life.

At the opposite end of the spectrum are the informal public spaces that exist no matter how little, if any, design is invested in them. The  street corner is the typical example of this pedestrian kind of public space. Thus one side contains those examples of extraordinary public spaces, which come to life on special occasions only; the other comprises the plurality of spaces which cater to the public on a daily basis, and usually both the space and the activities that take place are "infra-ordinary," to use Georges Perec's term. The extraordinary spaces are all unique in their own way, but almost interchangeable in their uniqueness; the infra-ordinary spaces are apparently all the same, but for the people who use them every day they have an undeniable singularity.

**Baana Pedestrian and Bicycle Corridor**
Helsinki City Planning Department,
HelsinkiPublic Works Department,
LociLandscape Architects
Helsinki, 2014

**Public Swimming Pool**
studioBasar
Bucharest, 2014

Both the extraordinary ceremonial spaces and infra-ordinary quotidian spaces can be found everywhere, from Brasília to Beijing, from Brisbane to Brazzaville, from Boston to Bangkok, and from Barcelona to Berlin. But what Barcelona, Berlin and every other European city also consist of—and what isn't so common in other parts of the world—is a very rich middle ground of public spaces that can be situated somewhere between the extraordinary and the infra-ordinary, offering neither the pomp and circumstance of the ceremonial public space nor anything else other than the mundaneness of the quotidian.

If there is a truly European aspect to public space it is to be found in its neighborhood parks and squares, playgrounds, green pockets, skateparks, bike lanes, pedestrian areas, basketball courts and all the regular urban spaces. And it does not even have to be a full space, it can be a couple of benches here, a few trees there, a well-positioned bicycle rack, street lighting, a water feature, a consistent street profile, a bus stop, a pavement, a public art work, or even markings on asphalt road surfaces that reveal that public space matters. This extends to the maintenance and care taken of it. In this respect, there is a parallel with architecture in Europe, which excels in a similar kind of middle ground, with all its collective housing, its schools and libraries, its sport facilities and community centers.

One reason why this middle ground exists in Europe in the first place is undeniably financial: dirt-poor nations can lavish huge resources on a single monumental square in front of the presidential palace (even if it would be better if they didn't), but only prosperous societies can afford this whole infrastructure of well-designed middle-ground public spaces (and architecture for that matter). Not every country that could pay for it is willing to do so, but in most European countries municipalities are. And they are usually the clients and financiers of public space. Or they manage to coerce project developers to pick up the tab as a condition for the permission to build. By doing so they manage to protect public space from the erosive powers of privatization, which were part and parcel of the pervasive political ideology of neoliberalism that led to the application of the logics of markets even in fields and disciplines where there is no real market. And despite huge technological changes that are deeply affecting everybody's understanding of public and private spheres, the hardware of the public space is still appreciated in Europe as essential to accommodating and generating a diversity of social interactions, expressions and gestures.

**Fountain Hacks**
LIKEarchitects. Ricardo Dourado
Porto, 2012

**Brandon Street Housing**
Metaphorm Architects
London, 2014

Because ultimately, no matter what the political color of national or municipal governments may be at any given moment, there is a European-wide consensus that public space contributes to the common good, and that the quality of public space can and does make a difference. This consensus is grounded in a very implicit yet fundamental belief in the values of democracy, and how they play out into public space. Even for people whose knowledge of Greek Antiquity goes no further than Plato and the Parthenon, there is some vague understanding of the possible relation between urban space and democracy, between the *agora* and the *polis,* in its double meaning of both the place and the people inhabiting it.

This kind of democratic middle-ground public space seems to flourish particularly in countries with the lowest income inequality, of which many are European. One tool to compare equality is the Gini index and, although there are several Gini indexes, all of which differ slightly from each other, what occurs is that the most equal countries in the world are almost all European. This correlation deserves a deeper analysis, but for the moment suffice it to say: "Show me your Gini and I will tell you what your public space looks like." Or the other way around: "Show me your public spaces and I can tell you how equal your society is."

Berlin and Barcelona are not randomly chosen to fit in the earlier alliterating enumeration of cities with names starting with a B. West Berlin of the Internationale Bauausstellung (IBA) in the 1980s, in what was then a still-divided Germany, and Barcelona in anticipation of the 1992 Olympic Games, in the first years of a new democratic Spain, are actually two crucial references when it comes to understanding the recent development of public space in Europe. Both reflect the postmodern turn of the European city: a reappraisal and rediscovery of forms of urbanity that rely not on the discontinuities and openness of modern planning but rather on finite and defined urban spaces and dense urban fabrics.

IBA Berlin and Olympic Barcelona are the starting points for the shortest possible history of public space in Europe, from the 1980s until the present. Berlin and Barcelona were the inspiration for many urban designers, mayors and civil servants in the 1990s, the 2000s and possibly even today. The reconstructed urban fabric of Berlin and the new squares and parks of Barcelona were examples of what turned out to be a contagious new faith in the city, a new confidence in urban culture. This resurgence of the city had its effect everywhere, from Hamburg to Turin, from Liverpool to Tirana, from Porto to Tallinn, from Oslo to Santa Cruz de Tenerife.

The brief history of the rediscovery of the city and of urban culture, this "triumph of the city" as Edward Glaeser has called it in his eponymous book, overlaps with the rapid ascent of the notion of public space, which had hitherto not entered professional parlance, as Thierry Paquot has noted in his concise L'espace public. Significant in terms of the still short life of the expression are the changes in the title of Jan Gehl's groundbreaking Life Between Buildings: Using Public Space, which is another important reference in this postmodern turn. When it was first published in Danish in 1971, the title was simply Livet mellem husene, "life between buildings," without any subtitle. The second Danish edition, which appeared nine years later, was given a subtitle: Udeaktiviteter og udemiljøer. This translates as "outdoor activities and outdoor environments:" no sign yet of public space. Only with the English translation of 1987 did the two words public and space appear on the cover and the title page. And subsequent translations in other languages included those words as well.

Before the 1980s "public space" was mainly used to describe the metaphorical public domain, of which newspapers, public opinion and democracy are examples. Paquot dwells on the difference in French between the plural and the singular form. The singular *espace public* refers to what he calls the "factory of public opinion." The plural form of *espaces publics* describes concrete urban spaces which, as Paquot convincingly shows, are not universal constants but differ from place to place and from period to period. They are not the same in Europe and, say, the Middle East, and today they are not the same as in medieval times.

Shortly after the first edition of Gehl's book appeared, another important publication came out which didn't use the term either but was also about public space, albeit from a formal perspective instead of a social one: Rob Krier's *Stadtraum in Theorie und Praxis* (1975). Both books target modernism and its shortcomings in producing public space, and offer a toolkit for making more meaningful spaces. In this respect, they are both truly postmodern.

These two publications fit into a wider postmodern discourse on the city and public space, which originated in the 1960s, gained traction in the 1970s and started to materialize in the built environment in the 1980s. This discourse was not limited to Europe only and was even seemingly dominated by American voices, such as Kevin Lynch (*The Image of the City*, 1960), Jane Jacobs (*The Death and Life of Great American Cities*, 1961), Erving Goffman (*Behavior in Public Places*, 1963), Colin Rowe and Fred Koetter (*Collage City*, 1978) and William Whyte (*The Social Life of Small Urban Places*, 1980), and later by the New Urbanists. But this says more about the role of English as the lingua franca, also in architecture and urbanism, than about the real center of gravity where these ideas on the city were put into practice, which was undoubtedly in Europe. Oriol Bohigas and MBM in Barcelona, Kleihues in Berlin, Aldo Rossi and his concept of the analogue city radiating from Milan, the morphological studies of Jean Castex and Philippe Panerai in Paris (*Formes urbaines: De l'îlot à la barre*, 1977), Rob and Léon Krier's pleas for the reconstruction of the European city, Maurice Culot's activist urban design in Brussels (with ARAU) and his curatorial work in Brussels and Paris, and Jan Gehl's studies and interventions in Copenhagen were just a few of the players who were active at the time.

The urban orientation of European postmodernism sets it apart from its American counterpart, which concentrated much more on architecture and symbolism. Obviously there were cross fertilizations of all kinds; by and large, however, the urban perspective was more extensively developed in Europe than anywhere else.

Zooming out from this short postmodern history, it is possible to paint a picture with broader brushstrokes in which recent public space is a continuation and outcome of a longer trend that started with the rapid urbanization everywhere in Europe during the nineteenth and early-twentieth centuries. This unprecedented urbanization started in England, the cradle of the Industrial Revolution, and reached Poland or Greece much later. But the general pattern was the same, with a societal shift from a predominantly rural culture to a predominantly urban culture.

This urbanization created not only what classical Marxism would term an "industrial proletariat" but also, and equally importantly, a new middle class of city dwellers. The correlation between this middle class, between the city and civil society, is as obvious as difficult to articulate. The nineteenth century witnessed a fundamental transformation of European societies with the rise of the middle class, which ultimately became not only the main user of the city, but directly or indirectly the client for it as well.

It is possible to write an even longer history of public space, which is usually abbreviated in a few sweeping statements about a connection if not a continuity leading from postmodern and modern times all the way back to the Roman forum and the Greek *stoa* and *agora*, making short stops at, for instance, the grandiose baroque squares in front of equally grandiose baroque churches in southern parts of Germany and Austria, the squares of the *palazzi civici* of Italian city-states and the market squares in medieval northern European cities. No matter how questionable this temporal triple jump may be, the very fact that it is possible to stretch back 2,500 years is indicative of the historical depth of public space in Europe, even during the very long period when it wasn't explicitly called public space.

Most of the chapters in this long history constitute nothing more than a solemn account of one kind of public space—the unique, ceremonial one—along with something on the infra-ordinary places that somehow survived demolition and oblivion. In a similar way, until the nineteenth century most of the historical architecture that survived, in reality or on the pages of history books, belonged either to infra-ordinary vernacular traditions or else were the exceptional palaces, cathedrals and temples and other monumental buildings.

**Parc de L'Estació del Nord**
Arriola & Fiol Arquitectes
Barcelona, 1988

**Parc del Clot**
Daniel Freixes, Vicente Miranda
Barcelona, 1986

When architecture began to gravitate from the exclusive domain of exceptional monuments for the ruling elite to building for civil society, urban planning shifted as well. In the nineteenth century, when urban planning as an independent profession was still in its infancy, it gradually moved away from the affirmative monumentality which sustained the power of a king, or the Church, to building cities for citizens, and by doing so, giving shape to society. The result might still be monumental, as we see from Hauss-mann's Parisian boulevards, Cerdà's urbanization of Barcelona, or Vienna's Ringstrasse, each of which were commissioned by the ruling powers. Yet these rulers were no longer only glorifying their own power; rather they were catering to the city and its citizens as well. Cerdà's repetitive structures of chamfered blocks in the Eixample offers the most striking example of the absence of conventional axial and directional monumentality, but also on the impressive Ringstrasse each part is commensurate to all the others, nullifying spatial hierarchies. The same is true of the boulevards of Paris, which imposed a new order on the city, and although they are monumental in themselves, in essence they are all equally important.

Back to postmodernism and the present. Compared to the transfor-mations in the nineteenth and early-twentieth centuries when many European cities changed and grew beyond recognition, the last few decades are certainly less dramatic, and less radically disruptive. Even the largest projects of recent times, like the London Docklands, Olympic and post-Olympic Barcelona, the Eastern Harbor Area in

**Reflections**

Amsterdam, Hamburg Hafen, the IBA and reunification of Berlin, Copenhagen Harbor or the Île de Nantes, are minor in relation to the scale of the city. Their physical impact, while still significant, is limited because they are more based on incremental changes than drastic make-overs. This is urbanism as "tinkering with a running engine," as Bernardo Secchi put it.

In this light, Berlin and Barcelona of the 1980s and 1990s marked a turning point not only after modernism but also after 150 years of rapid urbanization in Europe. Except for a very small number of outliers—London being the only one that comes to mind—it is unlikely that European cities will see substantial continuous growth. With a population that is only slowly increasing, a momentarily stagnating economy, and urbanization having reached saturation point, the future trend for many urban issues in Europe will probably be to remain downscaled from regional planning and building complete cities and districts to interventions on the level of a neighborhood, a block, a square or a street. This means it is quite likely that concern for public space is here to stay; indeed, it may even become more important than it already is.

**Hans Ibelings.** Architecture critic and historian. Cofounder of the magazine *A10 new European architecture*, he is presently editor of *The Architecture Observer*. Author of *European Architecture Since 1890* (2011).

"The continuous cities of Europe are engaged in a collective effort to bring flexibility into preexisting, ancient, and even prehistoric, contexts."

# Renovative Europe
## Teju Cole

Lagos is the city of my childhood and early adulthood; now I live
in New York City. The surprisingly similar models offered by these
two places shape my sense of our common urban life: frenetic,
somewhat aggressive, but also confident and relatively unburdened
by the detritus of history. Over the years, through many trips, I have
also become familiar with Europe. In *Invisible Cities*, Italo Calvino
used the term "continuous cities" to suggest that there is actually just
one big, continuous city that neither begins nor ends. "Only the name
of the airport changes," Calvino writes. And even the airports, I have
found, resemble each other to an uncanny degree; perhaps even more
than the city centers. Airports are, after all, the places where the
neurons of our modern life cluster most tightly.

Nevertheless, we also know that cities are distinct. Not only is
Barcelona one thing and Dakar another, we also know that there are
characteristics that Barcelona shares with Copenhagen, and Milan,
that make them, as a group, distinct from Dakar, Johannesburg, and
Nairobi. There are, in other words, sensible continental groupings,
based on a certain family resemblance.

What does that family resemblance look like in the case of European
cities? Experientially, I think of a certain cautiousness, of old stone-
work and new windows, of tasty dairy products, of the magnificent
cool of cathedrals, of wheat rather than rice. I think of the government's sense of responsibility towards the populace in terms of
education and healthcare, questions that are still up for debate in
Nigeria and the United States. Politically, I take a wider view: Europe
had relationships of conquest, trade, and plunder all across the
world—in the Americas, in the Near East, in Asia—but nowhere was
it as sustained as in Africa. Slavery and colonialism made Europe
rich at Africa's expense. In time, this circulation of goods and labor
altered somewhat. New complexities entered the picture: people migrated
in large numbers to where their goods had once gone. Precisely for
this reason, the European city is now a city of ethnic and economic
diversity, but also a city of vulnerability, tension, and sometimes hatred.

The most wretched wars in history happened on European soil. Rebuilding was transformative: postwar modernism layered onto the neo-classical, baroque, renaissance, medieval, and classical matrices of Europe. Stuttgart, Rotterdam, London, Milan, and Warsaw are all elaborations, in a sense, on this same set of variables. But even relatively undamaged places like Paris, Stockholm, and Basel moved according to the logic of renovation rather than of obliteration; they contain the same layers as bombed cities. I was struck, for instance, by the remarkable integration of old and new, in the design by David Chipperfield Architects of the Neues Museum in Berlin. I do not believe an American institution would have invited such a subtle and historically delicate intervention. This ethos of renovation in Europe is very much a philosophical project as well. This appears to be the case in Barcelona, where the energy of a strong but suppressed culture had to be renegotiated for a role on a national as well as continental scale. The same, perhaps, is true of Toulouse.

Lagos and New York, my two native cities, tend to build rather than rebuild, and they often build ahistorically. Reckless development is similarly the dominant tone in the enormous urban centers of south China and the Gulf States. But, in my view, Europe dances to a different melody: renovation and reconsideration are always part of the argument, even on a hitherto undeveloped site. The continuous cities of Europe are engaged in a collective effort to bring flexibility into preexisting, ancient, and even prehistoric, contexts.

But how does this flexibility fit into Europe's many current crises? These are hard times for Europe. The colonial legacy and its discontents are real. Islamic fundamentalism and neo-Nazism are twin horrors dragging violent threat in their wake, and both seem to defeat liberal, not to mention neoliberal, rationalizations. Turbulent economic rearrangements, attended by hubris and mercilessness, have brought misery to so many. There has been a shocking absence of memory, and thus a dereliction of duty, where refugees are concerned. Considering all this, one must agree with Zygmunt Bauman's idea of an ongoing interregnum in European philosophy: the great old ideas that helped make sense of modern life are waning in the face of new challenges, and the desperately needed new ideas are not established yet. It is an unsettled period. In the face of the dynamism of Chinese and Latin American cities, and in the face of the potential energy of African cities, do European cities still have anything to offer the world?

I would suggest that the Enlightenment is not over yet. The cities of Europe, in addition to their inexhaustible beauty, can serve as laboratories for how things could be, an alternative future that does not follow the model of Dubai. This is because of that special pressure of having to renovate, instead of being at liberty to throw it all away and start anew. Renovative thinking—architecturally, but also economically and politically—combined with the breadth of cosmopolitan experience, can make European cities an essential player in the sustainable model on which the future of the planet depends. "Old Europe," as the American warlord Donald Rumsfeld dismissively referred to it more than a decade ago, could have a lot to teach the younger, narrower world yet.

**Teju Cole.** Writer, photographer and art historian. Author of *Open City* (2011).

"No longer blueprint, the European city becomes the destination of other desires—of tourism, for sure, but also of escape, maybe nostalgia."

# From Blueprints to Alter-Spaces

## Teresa Caldeira

The European City and the Latin American City do not exist. But
we imagine them all the time. These imaginaries tend to be simplistic
and homogenizing, but they are productive. They have shaped
desires, perceptions, actions, and cities themselves. Nevertheless,
they seem also to have grown farther apart in recent times, as the
European city becomes evanescent when viewed from the perspective of the everydayness of the southern metropolises.

From the very beginning, hierarchy has structured urban imagin-
ings between the two sides of the Atlantic. Back in the sixteenth
century, The Law of the Indies established the blueprint of cities to
be built all over Spanish America, not infrequently overlaying cities
of preexisting peoples. Colonial cities continued to be conceived
according to European models for centuries. Even after imperial
powers were formally gone, cities and their citizens looked at
the capitals of the Empire for guidance on how to build and organize
cities. French boulevards proliferated, and Haussmann's interventions in nineteenth-century Paris were replicated in cities of Latin
America that aspired to the status of modernity. Thus, for centuries,
imaginaries traveled one way from North to South, and European
urban principles shaped plans for southern cities yet to come. European cities were admired and idealized: vibrant streets and public
spaces, beauty and order, sites of sophisticated consumption, historical
depth, politeness, civilized encounters—all that Latin American
cities seemed to lack.

In the mid-twentieth century, things started to change in interesting
ways, as modernist imaginaries, definitively European in origin,
were adopted to create modernist cities from scratch in Latin America.
These new cities were expected to propel a radical transformation/
modernization of the nations of the South that would set them on

their own independent paths. As is usually the case, things did not happen exactly as planned. But as Latin American cities embarked on plans of modernization, the gaps that have always existed between cities north and south and inside both types acquired new meanings and forms.

Brasília is probably the archetype of these modernist projects. Although it realized its designers' intentions in some ways, in many it never did. Nevertheless, modernism and modernization changed all large Latin American cities in ways that divorced them from their previous European imaginaries. Modernism became the main aesthetic of Latin American elites and the central spaces they occupy in many cities. In Europe, however, while modernist architecture has also carried its signs of prestige, modernist urbanism has reigned especially in peripheries, where the superblocks produced after the end of World War II structured the territories of many working classes, from the French *banlieues* to the outskirts of countless eastern European cities. Their centers retained an older premodernist fabric; their peripheries became modernist.

By contrast, city centers in Latin America tore down their colonial foundations to erect modernist structures on the ruins. Moreover, their peripheries, usually far away from the modern cores, were spared modernist superblocks until recently due to the incapacity of both state and elites to produce the territories of the working classes. Residents themselves created these spaces according to a relatively unregulated process known as autoconstruction. They acquired and/or occupied land in far away hinterlands and took at least one generation to build their own individual houses and to urbanize their neighborhoods. The logic of this production is not imported from Europe or inspired by distant models. But it is shared everywhere in the global South by poor urban citizens who can inhabit cities only if they directly produce them. The results are low density and disperse territories of uneven quality and much creativity; territories of poor residents who frequently have legitimate claims to the ownership of their residences but who, for various reasons, cannot get title; territories of citizens who, in the process of creating their spaces, transformed themselves into political subjects and become fluent in rights talk.

These segregated, highly unequal, and autoconstructed cities of Latin America no longer turn to Europe for models. Their elites may still look at cities in the United States for inspiration, investigating how US Americans plan and build large projects such as shopping malls, sports and entertainment centers, and science and technology parks. The vast urban peripheries of Latin America, however, became something else; spaces that cannot be subsumed in either the analytical models or the lived experiences of cities of the North Atlantic. Latin American cities throughout the continent now belong to another urban species.

Thus, seen from the point of view of contemporary Latin American urban spaces, European cities look like alter-territories. Their long and layered histories, dense yet compact scale, corridor streets and well-cared-for public spaces, and even their patterns of segregation seem too disconnected from the realities of most large Latin American cities. This thick alterity blocks the circulation of imaginaries. No longer blueprint, the European city becomes the destination of other desires—of tourism, for sure, but also of escape, maybe nostalgia. Although these distant and divergent paths are dominant, cities on both sides of the Atlantic converge in one important area: youth culture. Thus, they both have walls and doors covered by graffiti. Young people north and south seem to appropriate their city spaces not through common plans to order them, but rather through a media-inspired and shared repertoire of actions, images, movements, and sounds to mark them. Yet today there is a new difference: youth in the North are now also looking closely at youth in the South to fuel their imaginations.

**Teresa Caldeira.** Anthropologist. Professor of City and Regional Planning at the University of California, Berkeley. Author of *City of Walls: Crime, Segregation and Citizenship in São Paulo* (2000).

"From Baudelaire to
Benjamin, the ability
to stroll has been identified
as key to cosmopolitan
modernity and a vibrant
public sphere."

# Ambulatory Urbanism

## Diane E. Davis

The more intimate and pedestrian-friendly streetscapes of European cities stand in contrast to most American cities, where infinitely expanding roadways, convoluted traffic interchanges, and the supremacy of the private automobile have structured urban grids and made walkability the exception more than the rule. The implications of automobile dominance for public space are disconcerting. A city where citizens whisk through space at speeds and latitudes that separate them from face-to-face encounters will not easily find opportunities for begetting publicity or a truly engaged sociality. From Baudelaire to Benjamin, the ability to stroll has been identified as key to cosmopolitan modernity and a vibrant public sphere. Yet, the urban condition as experienced from the vantage point of a car is a far cry from the intimate social interaction that comes when individuals meet in serendipitous encounters on streets, in parks, or in structures repurposed for collective mingling and exploration. It is not for nothing that the American author Cornelia Otis Skinner once proclaimed that the concept of the *flâneur* had no counterpart in the Anglo-American world.[1] While European cities host a wide array of public spaces that make rambling and other ambulatory forms of social encounter both familiar and memorable, American cities tend to lack the infrastructures that encourage such occurrences. This sad fact should inspire American urban designers to learn from abroad, to question the social correlates of our urban built environments, and to work more creatively to produce socially vibrant public spaces. Rethinking the opportunities for pedestrian mobility and how it can be enhanced in cities dominated by cars is the first step in achieving such aims.

1 Cornelia Otis Skinner, *Elegant Wits and Grand Horizontals*. (New York: Houghton Mifflin, 1962).

Many European cities count on the advantages of history to explain why they lead the world in producing or preserving walkability. The layout of streets and edifices that make possible a wide range of ambulatory encounters in public space can be partly traced to historical developments that established the contours of the urban built environment in European cities long before the advent of the car. But more than a mere physical legacy, the social and spatial history of European cities has reinforced a cultural valuing and aesthetic appreciation of public spaces, apparent in the proliferation of arcades, plazas, parks, or other promenades that came to define European cities early on. In North America, political fear of the collective fervor of the masses has long been a fetter to the creation of such spaces. For much of the nineteenth and twentieth centuries, America's major cities were identified as hosting the "dangerous classes," comprised of immigrants, the poor, the industrial working class, and other culturally, socially, and politically marginalized populations feared by both elites and middle classes. City leaders often dreaded the possibility of their collective organization. If such populations were able to gather easily in public spaces, they might demand revolution. A metropolis without public spaces was a controllable city, a quiet city, a politically disabled city.

The legacy of this perspective is apparent even today. New York City, perhaps America's most public and socially inclusive metropolis, does indeed have Central Park thanks to the great urban reformer and landscape architect Frederick Law Olmsted. But it also hosts a plethora of private gated parks and other "privately-owned public spaces," of which the much-celebrated Zuccotti Park is merely one. When America's Occupy movement chose that small triangle of concrete to launch their assault on the privilege and dominance of the nation's banking elite, they also revealed the fact that the city had very few open spaces that were truly public. Protestors had to deal with legal constraints on their rights to gather in particular city spaces, and not merely with the larger issues of injustice that instigated the mobilization in the first place. Yet all is not lost. New York City's most fêted public space these days is a reconfigured high-way overpass called the High Line, whose existence demonstrates that there are movements afoot to recover streets and roadways for citizens. It may be poetic justice that such advances have been achieved by slowly chipping away at automobile dominance, symbolically if not in actuality. Building on this momentum, the High Line was soon followed by New York City's expansion of pedestrian streets, a new bike-share program, and a range of other policies to recover the social power of the street by allowing individuals to move through public space at a much more human speed.

The challenge that lies ahead will involve major efforts to construct or recast physical infrastructures in ways that bring ambulatory urbanism to American cities, using such projects to foster greater appreciation of public sociability. Innovations in urban space that bring citizens together while simultaneously challenging the car culture must be at the forefront of this agenda. There is much to learn from European cities in this regard. But Americans must also accommodate and invent their own vernacular. Highways will not easily disappear, a city grid formed for automobile accessibility is difficult to subvert, and the seductive lure of individual freedom that cars provide is a difficult beast to tame.

**Diane E. Davis.** Sociologist. Charles Dyer Norton Professor of Regional Planning and Urbanism at the Graduate School of Design, Harvard University. Coeditor of *Cities and Sovereignty: Identity Politics in Urban Spaces* (2011).

"We need to find a new language with which to give an account of the conversation that modern cities have long held with each other, or certain conversations they've refused to hold."

# The European City and Memory

## Amit Chaudhuri

I began to discover the European city early in the new millennium. Not that I hadn't known or seen European cities before. I'd lived between London, Oxford, and Cambridge from 1983 to 1999; I'd visited Paris twice in the nineties, and had also been to Spain and Belgium on literary invitations. In fact, I first went to London, Paris, and Rome with my parents on a combination of a holiday and a medical tour in 1973 (my father wanted my heart murmur to be examined by a Harley Street doctor). Evidently, I'd seen a lot but also seen little: my experience of the city was mediated for me probably by some generic idea handed down by Hollywood or television, or even the incessant, boring rhetoric to do with categories such as "First World" and "Third World," "East" and "West." Still, by my second trip to Spain in 1999, I'd begun to realize that "Europe" seemed quite distinct from "England," just as regions within England were unlike each other. Within Spain, for instance, there was a variety of registers when it came to location. Gijón, in the North, was different from the southern cities of Madrid and, especially, Alcalá de Henares (Cervantes's birthplace), where the marks of the Ottoman Empire were striking. The economically depressed city, Valladolid, presented another category altogether of the European town. Provincial townsmen who'd gathered at my hotel for an early dinner on the evening I arrived there, their hair oiled and their shirts neatly pressed, demonstrating a subterranean awareness of never having seen anyone like me in the flesh before, reminded me of Bengalis congregating in the historic but neglected Coffee House of North Calcutta, on College Street. Calcutta was once an international metropolis, and the Coffee House an intellectual hub; by now, however, they've both been three decades in decline, and the neighborhoods of North Calcutta are derelict. It was a particular progression, or unraveling of history, that brought an echo of Calcutta to Valladolid that evening: deceptive gentility close to despair. My visits to Berlin in 2004 and 2005 crystallized for me the fact that I felt a curious intimacy in Europe, an inkling of the past and of history, such as I'd never experienced in England. What prompted this process of recognition and recall in European cities?

To take the example of Calcutta: the landowners' mansions that came up in North Calcutta from the end of the eighteenth century of course combined Bengali design with features from the European Renaissance, like Corinthian pillars. From the late-nineteenth century to the 1950s, a new kind of middle-class house began to come up in, and increasingly constitute, Calcutta's neighborhoods, with red oxide stone floors, long verandahs, green slatted windows (these actually go back to the eighteenth century or earlier), an unexpected variety of grille-work, open rooftop terraces, intricate cornices and ironwork on balcony railings, perforations on the sides of walls, serving as vents, each different from building to building, and the houses themselves— although they shared these elements—built to a multiplicity of unrepeatable designs. The mix of these elements—so natural to the habitat that they are hardly noticed—is surprising, but not their provenance, given the French, Dutch, and Portuguese interest in Bengal from as early as the seventeenth century. Add to this, more recently, the response to Art Deco in the 1940s and 1950s: the houses with semicircular balconies and porthole-windows. All this makes Calcutta so unlike London. Not only the buildings, the streets in Calcutta's residential areas were made to accommodate the passer-by, the pedestrian, and the person who's elected to lose their way in a manner that's more European than English. Another fact: the Indian middle classes, like the European, but unlike the British, often live in apartments rather than houses; and both Europeans and Indians (again, unlike the English) seem to prefer dwellings with balconies. Given that European cities themselves, as they grew, would have borrowed characteristics from the Middle East, Asia, and further afield, the categories of East and West seem of less and less use, and the term "European" richer and more problematic than we think. It certainly brings an end to conventional colonial history as a way of describing Calcutta. And it explains to some extent the alienation I used to feel in London, and the incongruous stirrings of recognition and recall I experienced on the streets of Berlin, Geneva, and Istanbul.

Over the last two and a half years I've been arguing for ways
to hang on to these Calcutta houses, which are rapidly vanishing.
Comparisons have come up; I've mentioned Berlin more than
once. I've been reprimanded: you can't compare eastern cities to
western, I'm told, or developing cities to developed ones. But we
need to find a new language with which to give an account of the
conversation that modern cities have long held with each other,
or certain conversations they've refused to hold. Dubai, for instance,
is an "eastern" city that has the ethos of a first-world one, and
yet has less similarity with either Bombay ("eastern") or Berlin
("first-world") than with Dallas or Atlanta. The latter resemble
Kuala Lumpur more than they do New York, which, in turn, was once,
before it was deliberately packaged, reminiscent of Calcutta and
Berlin. Our visits to cities teach us something: that the way we respond
to what's familiar and what's foreign (were we to bother to inquire
into these responses), and often realign the two, is more revealing
than what either tour guides or history books tell us.

**Amit Chaudhuri.** Writer. Professor of Contemporary Literature at the University of East Anglia.
Author of *Calcutta: Two Years in the City* (2013) and *Odysseus Abroad* (2015).

"We currently inhabit what in all likelihood is an irrevocably and irreversibly multicultural world, a product of the massive migration of ideas, values and beliefs, as well as of their human carriers."

# Cities in the Globalized World of Diasporization

## Zygmunt Bauman

Public spaces in the city, which allow free access to everybody while attracting and encouraging the city residents to make use of the facilities put at their disposal, are urban variations of "commons." As Jeremy Rifkin recently reminded us,[1] commons predate modern capitalist institutions and are in fact "the oldest form of institutionalized, self-managed activity in the world." He goes on to explain very briefly how the starting and arrival points of the current transformation differ: "While the capitalist market is based on self-interest and driven by material gain, the social Commons is motivated by collaborative interests and driven by a deep desire to connect with others and share. If the former promotes property rights, *caveat emptor*, and the search for autonomy, the latter advances open-source innovation, transparency, and the search for community."

In fact, the last comment invokes another historical root of urban public spaces: the ancient Greek *agora*, a place set aside for regular gatherings of the citizens who were entitled—and also obliged—to partake in the running of city affairs. In concept as well as in practice, the *agora* was the place meant to simultaneously reproduce each citizen's individual autonomy and the integrity of their community; a place of incessant two-directional translation of diverse individual interests, rights and duties merged with common policies and the needs of the community. Inside the ancient *polis*, simultaneously a city and a state, the *agora* fulfilled the function from which the modern nation-state—determined by the concentration and monopolization of power over its sovereign territory—was to strive to expropriate the public spaces of the cities. But by now, in the era

1 Jeremy Rifkin, *The Zero Marginal Cost Society: The Internet of Things, the Collaborative Commons, and the Eclipse of Capitalism* (New York: Palgrave Macmillan, 2014), 16.

of global interdependency, the concept of the State's territorial sovereignty is fast becoming an illusion. Furthermore, the assumed sovereignty of the individual to which states defer in order to excuse themselves from the function they are incapable of fulfilling, due to their acute power deficit, had been an illusion from birth: a figment of the imagination of governments keen to dismiss the protective obligations of the State. Therefore, for different reasons, the actors operating at levels above and below the in-between "medium level" of social integration are equally unfit for the job. It is to that medium level that the eyes of many people eager to preserve or restore the regular encounters and mutual support between individual autonomy and communal integration are currently turning.

The "medium level" of societal integration is, of course, a fairly vast territory, densely populated and encompassing a variegated multitude of actors. Not all of them are promising enough to deserve investing hopes in them for the resurrection of an effective agency of collective action. However, I am inclined to follow the trail blazed by Benjamin Barber in his provocative and convincing manifesto published last year by Yale University Press under the title *If Mayors Ruled the World: Dysfunctional Nations, Rising Cities*. "Today," states Barber, "after a long history of regional success, the nation-state is failing us on the global scale. It was the perfect political recipe for the liberty and independence of autonomous peoples and nations. It is utterly unsuited to interdependence. The city, always the human habitat of first resort, has in today's globalizing world once again become democracy's best hope."

Why are nation-states singularly unfit to tackle the challenges arising from our planet-wide interdependence? Because being "too inclined by their nature to rivalry and mutual exclusion," nation-states appear "quintessentially indisposed to cooperation and incapable of establishing global common goods." Why are cities, especially big cities, immensely more adapted to take the lead? Because of "the unique urban potential for cooperation and egalitarianism unhindered by those obdurate forces of sovereignty and nationality, of ideology and inequality, that have historically hobbled and isolated nation-states inside fortresses celebrated as being 'independent' and 'autonomous'. Nor need the mayors tie their aspirations to cooperation to the siren song of a putative United Nations that will never be united because it is composed of rival nations whose essence lies in their sovereignty and independence." In fact, as Barber emphatically points out, far from being a utopian fantasy, this is already happening: unplanned, unsupervised, and unmonitored. It happens spontaneously, as a natural phase in the development of cities as locations where "creativity is unleashed, community solidified, and citizenship realized." Confronted daily by globally generated problems and the urge to resolve them, cities are already proving their ability to address "multiplying problems of an interdependent world" incomparably quicker and better than the offices of nation-state capitals. To cut a long story short: "Cities have little choice: to survive and flourish they must remain hospitable to pragmatism and problem solving, to cooperation and networking, to creativity and innovation." So, if you wish, this marks out the way to the *polis*, a sort of "city-state" big enough to render its policies effective yet compact enough to involve, stimulate and engage its population in setting goals and monitoring their pursuit.

One of the numerous globally-generated problems with which local authorities—big cities prominent among them—have been confronted point-blank and saddled with the task of searching for solutions is the socio-cultural outcome of massive "diasporization" of the urban territory. The early-modern policy of "assimilation" being no longer either plausible or desired, migrants arriving nowadays at the already densely populated cities (for the first time in history, the majority of humans reside in such urban places) are neither willing, nor pushed, nor ordered to "assimilate," that is, to renounce their identities and particular life styles; rather, they retain their differences. For this reason, contemporary migration creates scattered yet closely connected islands of distinct cultural identities. This present-day migration is massive and, notwithstanding the noises made by politicians keen on electoral profits, bound to grow. Michel Agier, the foremost researcher on the nature and consequences of mass migration, warns that current estimates presage one billion "displaced persons" in the next forty years. "After globalization of capitals, commodities and images, the time for globalization of humanity has finally arrived."[2] But the displaced are people with no place of their own and no place they can legitimately claim. As Agier points out,

---

2 Michel Agier, *Le couloir des exilés: Être étranger dans un monde commun.* (Bellecombe-en-Bauges: Éd. du Croquant, 2011), 95.

the journey itself, conducted with no clear point of arrival, makes "no-place" their indefinitely durable place: they lack a place in the common world, so to speak. The most common reaction of the natives of the lands they attempt to join is the demand for "integration *into*," not "integration *with*," "a nation-state as a pseudo-ethical imagined community;"[3] to put it bluntly, a demand to "submit to a predefined whole" while shedding and shredding their own identities, something they are reticent to do or all too often prevented from doing by the very same natives. Close daily proximity of different ethnicities, religions, languages, collective memories, and historically formed modes of life creates an ambience of anxiety and mutual suspicion.

A "stranger," by definition, is an unfamiliar being and, for that reason, a carrier of uncertainty and a vague, under-defined threat difficult to pinpoint: a stranger is an *a priori* suspicious creature, guilty until proven innocent (or rather until proving himself guiltless and having such proof accepted). In our liquid-modern society, smarting under the perpetual fear of losing one's place in society, of exclusion, of falling out or banishment, the migrants—nomads out of necessity even if sedentary in their dreams and intentions—are, in addition, "walking dystopias" that bring the specter of enforced uprooting close to already unsafe homes. The combined psychological effect is "mixo-phobia," the horror of mixing and the urge for territorial separation, which as a rule acquires a self-reinforcing momentum of its own. The less the members of different diasporized communities associate and communicate with each other, the less they develop skills of conversing, the ability of mutual understanding and the will to meet, associate and team up; a state of mind and emotions which in turn intensifies mutual mistrust and fear, prompting them to expand and deepen. The opportunity of "mixophilia"—an inclination toward face to face, point blank, earnest and sincere encounters leading to a meaningful dialogue and mutual comprehension, fusion of horizons and reciprocal spiritual enrichment—is in danger of being lost. A danger though by no means a necessity. As a matter of fact, mixing with difference has multiple attractions and holds quite a few tempting promises. Mixophilic tendencies, fostered by sharing the streets, workplaces, schools, and public spaces of the city, are never stifled completely: they may only go underground in times of occasional, unpreventable inflammations of mutual mistrust and

---

3 Gerd Baumann, "*Nation, Ethnicity and Community*", in Kim Knott and Seán McLoughlin, *Diasporas: Concepts, Intersections, Identities.* (London: Zed Books, 2010), 47.

grievance. The impacts of the two psychological responses to the same condition of urban life are finely balanced; it is virtually impossible to presage which of the two is set to prevail and for how long. We do face risks and opportunities in one indivisible package deal. Here you are: take it or leave it.

We currently inhabit what in all likelihood is an irrevocably and irreversibly multicultural world, a product of the massive migration of ideas, values and beliefs, as well as of their human carriers. Physical separation, if still conceivable (a moot question), no longer assures spiritual distance. "Their God" and "ours" have their respective temples built in each other's immediate neighborhoods, although inside the online universe in which we all spend an already considerable and growing chunk of our waking time, all temples are located at the same distance or, more to the point, in the same space-time proximity. However, we should be careful to set apart the two notions all too often misleadingly interchanged in public vocabulary: multiculturality and multiculturalism. The first denotes realities (of surroundings, life-scenes, ambience), while the second refers to an attitude, policy, or life-strategy of choice. In his most recent oeuvre Piotr Nowak, one of the most compelling Polish philosophers,[4] subjects Stanley Fish—the *enfant terrible* of the sedate scholarship establishment—to a thorough vivisection of his critique of the second of the multiculturalist attitudes and/or programs.[5]

Fish distinguishes two varieties of multiculturalism: "boutique" and "strong." The first is marked by the jarring contradiction between, on the one hand, the "politically correct" principles which (in Nowak's words) "emphasize the importance of proper relations between coexisting cultures as well as the respect and sympathy allegedly bestowed upon them" and, on the other, the fact that such principles throttle "the rage and allergy aroused by the genuine disparities found vexing and offending." And "boutique multiculturalism"—wrongly convinced of its universality and appearing to be dedicated to the principles of tolerance, neutrality, impartiality, open-mindedness and fairness—fails to comprehend those who take their convictions and life routines seriously, however idiosyncratic and repulsive they may be, clinging to them rigidly and devotedly.

4 Piotr Nowak, *Hodowanie troglodytów (Breeding Troglodytes)*. (Warsaw: Fundacja Augusta Hrabiego Cieszkowskiego, 2014).
5 Stanley Fish, "Boutique Multiculturalism, or Why Liberals Are Incapable of Thinking about Hate Speech", in *Critical Inquiry* 23, no. 2 (winter, 1997), 378–395; and *The Problem with Principle*, (Cambridge: Harvard UP, 1999).

The second, "strong," version of multiculturalism goes the whole hog, so to speak: it accords every culture an infrangible and indisputable right to practice whatever it considers right and proper, as well as barring all external critique let alone interference of the practices this or that culture promotes. Both versions, though, share the same original sin: like Pontius Pilate they wash their hands of the genuine differences, conflicts and frictions. By letting them "stew in their own juice," they acquire their own self-propelled, morbid and, in the long run, catastrophic momentum, which derives from the refusal to recognize and face such differences, conflicts and frictions point-blank in order to engage in a dialogue based on mutual comprehension and on the will to negotiate a mutually acceptable *modus co-vivendi*.

Strategies can be and are many and different, but one thing is crystal clear: the policy of mutual separation, keeping one's distance, building walls instead of bridges, and settling for tight sound-insulated "echo-chambers" instead of hotlines of real-time communication—and in general manifesting one's indifference under the disguise of toler-ance—leads nowhere other than to the wasteland of estrangement and aggravation. Chasing the challenge out of sight produces a deceptive comfort that in the short run myopically stores explosives for future detonations. And so one conclusion is equally crystal clear: the sole way out of the present discomfort and future woes is through the rejection of the treacherous temptations of separation; indeed, making such separation unfeasible by dismantling the border posts and bringing the annoying differences, dissimilarities, and self-imposed estrangements into a close, daily and increasingly intimate contact, hopefully resulting in a *fusion* instead of the self-propelling and self-exacerbating *fission* of horizons.

So here we are: the crucial role that urban public spaces are called upon (indeed, anointed!) to play is by far the greatest challenge (in fact the "meta-challenge," the one that needs to be faced in order to face all the other challenges) and the greatest task (indeed the "meta-task") of our times: the resurrection and survival of a true-to-its-vocation community, democracy, human solidarity and coopera-tion, and thereby raising the bar of human cohabitation to the rank of "collaborative commons." There is no guarantee of the full and final success of public spaces; even less of the instant and immediately tangible effects of their labor. It is in the light of this predicament and these prospects that the CCCB's initiative to monitor the fate of public spaces and fully investigate their developing potential acquires such tremendous significance, as well as bringing the results of their fifteen-year-long research to the people whose future depends on public spaces' ongoing story; that is, to all of us.

**Zygmunt Bauman.** Sociologist and writer. Professor Emeritus of Sociology at the University of Leeds and the University of Warsaw. Author of *Europe: An Unfinished Adventure* (2004) and *Liquid Times: Living in an Age of Uncertainty* (2006).

# Credits

PHOTO Pawel Kubisztal

**Huéscar**, Spain
**Tower of Homage**
2000–2007
DEVELOPER Government
of Andalucia / AUTHOR Antonio
Jiménez Torrecillas / PHOTO Jesús
Granada
**Special Mention 2008**

**Zadar**, Croatia
**Renovation of the Petar Zoranić
Square**
2009–2013
DEVELOPER City Council of Zadar
AUTHORS Aleksandra Krebel,
Alan Kostren#ić / PHOTO Damir
Fabijanic
**Finalist 2014**

**Krakow**, Poland
**Heroes of the Ghetto Square**
2003–2005
DEVELOPER City of Krakow
AUTHORS Biuro Projektow Lewicki
Latak, Piotr Lewicki & Kazimierz
Latak / PHOTO Pawel Kubisztal
**Special Mention 2006**

**Nantes**, France
**Memorial to the Abolition
of Slavery**
2003–2011
DEVELOPER Nantes Metropole, City
of Nantes / AUTHORS Wodiczko +
Bonder, architecture, art & design
PHOTO Philippe Ruault
**Special Mention 2012**

**Barcelona**, Spain
**Restoration of the Turó
de la Rovira**
2009–2011
DEVELOPER Barcelona City Council
AUTHORS Jansana, de la Villa, de
Paauw arquitectes, AAUP Jordi
Romero i associats, History of the
City Museum / PHOTO Lourdes
Jansana
**Joint Winner 2012**

**Kalmar**, Sweden
**Stortorget**
1999–2003
DEVELOPER Swedish Arts Council
AUTHORS Caruso St John
Architects, Eva Löfdahl / PHOTO
Hélène Binet
**Special Mention 2004**

**Berlin**, Germany
**Tilla Durieux Park**
1999–2003
DEVELOPER Municipality of Berlin
AUTHORS Jana Crepon, Bruno
Doedens, Ingo Golz, Merijn
Groenhart, Harma Horlings, Willem
Jan Snel, Maike van Stiphout,
DS Landschapsarchitecten / PHOTO
DS Lansdschapsarchitecten
**Special Mention 2004**

**Altach**, Austria
**Islamic Cemetery**
2007–2012
DEVELOPER City Council of Altach
AUTHOR Bernardo Bader Architects
PHOTO Adolf Bereuter
**Special Mention 2014**

**Folkestone**, United Kingdom
**Other People's Photographs**
2005–2008
DEVELOPER / AUTHOR / PHOTO
Strange Cargo Arts Company
**Special Mention 2008**

PHOTO Tania Ruiz

**Helsinki**, Finland
**Baana Pedestrian and Bicycle
Corridor**
2003–2012
DEVELOPER Helsinki City Executive
Office / AUTHORS Helsinki City
Planning Department, Helsinki
Public Works Department,
Loci Landscape Architects
PHOTO Krista Muurinen
**Special Mention 2014**

**Teruel**, Spain
**Refurbishment of the Paseo
del Óvalo**
2000–2003
DEVELOPER Government
of Aragon / AUTHORS David
Chipperfield architects, b720
Arquitectos, Fermín Vázquez
PHOTO Hisao Susuki
**Joint Winner 2004**

**Dublin**, Ireland
**Smithfield Esplanade**
1997–2000
DEVELOPER Dublin Corporation
AUTHORS McGarry Ní Éanaigh
Architects
PHOTO Dave Meehan
**Joint Winner 2000**

**Robbiano**, Italy
**Black Square, White Square**
2002–2005
DEVELOPER Municipality of
Giussano / AUTHORS Ifdesign,
Ida Origgi, Chiara Toscani

PHOTO Franco Tagliabue
**Special Mention 2006**

**London**, United Kingdom
**Reform of Exhibition Road**
2009–2011
DEVELOPER Royal Borough of
Kensington and Chelsea
AUTHOR Dixon Jones Architects
PHOTO Royal Borough of
Kensington and Chelsea
**Special Mention 2012**

**Malmö**, Sweden
**Elsewhere**
2004–2010
DEVELOPERS Information
Technology Malmö, National
Public Art, Public Transport
Administration
AUTHOR / PHOTO Tania Ruiz
**Special Mention 2012**

**Amsterdam**, Netherlands
**LED Cloud**
2010–2013
DEVELOPER Amsterdam-Noord
Borough / AUTHOR Sophie Valla
PHOTO Marcus Koppen
**Selected 2014**

**Buenavista del Norte**, Spain
**Green Tenerife**
1999–2002
DEVELOPER Government of Tenerife
AUTHORS Félix Perera, Urbano
Yanes, GPY Arquitectos
PHOTO Joaquín Ponce de León
**Special Mention 2004**

**Wroclaw**, Poland
**Integrated Tram & Train Stop**
2008–2012
DEVELOPERS Wroclawskie
Inwestycje / AUTHORS Maćków
Pracownia Projektowa / PHOTO
Maćków Pracownia Projektowa
**Selected 2014**

**Elx**, Spain
**The Braided Valley**
2009–2013
DEVELOPER Municipality of Elx
AUTHORS Francisco Leiva Ivorra,
Marta García Chico, Antoni Baile
Jiménez, Prócoro del Real Baeza
PHOTO Jesús Granada
**Joint Winner 2014**

PHOTO Jani Peternelj

**Innsbruck**, Austria
**Centrum Odorf**
2001–2006
DEVELOPER IIG Innsbrucker
Immobilien Gesmbh / AUTHOR
Froetscher Lichtenwagner / PHOTO
Lukas Schaller
**Special Mention 2008**

**Copenhagen**, Denmark
**Superkilen**
2008–2012
DEVELOPER Realdania, Municipality
of Copenhagen / AUTHOR BIG
Bjarke Ingels Group, Superflex,
Topotek 1 / PHOTO Iwan Baan
**Selected 2012**

**Mollet del Vallès**, Spain
**Can Mulà Multipurpose Center**
1991–2000
DEVELOPER Municipality of Mollet
del Vallès / AUTHORS Jordi
Cartagena, Enric Serra, Lluís Vives,
Serra-Vives-Cartagena / PHOTO
Joan Argelés Cugat, Lluís Casals
**Joint Winner 2000**

**Rotterdam**, Netherlands
**Urban Activator**
2005–2009
DEVELOPERS Foundation
'Grotekerkplein', OBR Rotterdam,
Rotary Club Rotterdam Noord
AUTHOR Atelier Kempe Thill
PHOTO Ulrich Schwarz
**Special Mention 2010**

**Espinho**, Portugal
**Marinha de Silvade
Urban Rehabilitation**
1996–2002
DEVELOPER Municipality of Espinho
AUTHORS João Paulo Júnior, Carlos
A. Sárria, Carlos Alberto Silva
PHOTO Carlos A. Sárria
**Special Mention 2002**

**Ljubljana**, Slovenia
**Riverside Refurbishment**
2004–2011
DEVELOPERS Municipality of
Ljubljana, Ljubljana Tourist
Office, Energy Service Company,
Carniolan Investment Company
AUTHORS Atelier Arhitekti,
Atelje Vozli⊕, BB Arhitekti,
Boris Podrecca, Dans arhitekti,
Medprostor, Trije arhitekti, Urbi
PHOTO Breda Bizjak
**Joint Winner 2012**

**Tirana**, Albania
**I Like Playing! 100 Playgrounds**
2007–2008
DEVELOPER Municipality of
Tirana / AUTHOR FUSHA
PHOTO Municipality of Tirana
**Finalist 2008**

**Rotterdam**, Netherlands
**Westblaak Skatepark**
1998–2001
DEVELOPER dS+V Gemeente
Rotterdam / AUTHOR Dirk van
Peijpe / PHOTO dS+V Gemente
Rotterdam
**Special Mention 2002**

**London**, United Kingdom
**Barking Town Square**
2005–2008
DEVELOPER London Borough of
Barking and Dagenham
AUTHORS Allford Hall Monaghan
and Morris, muf architecture/art
PHOTO muf architecture/art
**Joint Winner 2008**

PHOTO Peter Beard_LANDROOM

**Credits**

**Barcelona**, Spain
**Environmental Refurbishment
of the Besòs River Area**
1996–2000
DEVELOPER / AUTHORS / PHOTO
Barcelona Regional
**Special Mention 2002**

**Zuera**, Spain
**Regeneration of the Gállego River
and Surroundings**
1999–2001
DEVELOPER Municipality
of Zuera / AUTHORS aldayjover
Arquitectura y Paisaje,
Iñaki Alday, Margarita Jover,
María Pilar Sancho
PHOTO Jordi Bernadó
**Joint Winner 2002**

**Zaanstadt**, Netherlands
**A8ernA**
2003–2005
DEVELOPER Municipality of
Zaanstadt / AUTHORS Pieter
Bannenberg, Walter Van Dijk,
Kamiel Klaasse, Mark Linnemann,
NL Architects / PHOTO Luuk
Kramer
**Joint Winner 2006**

**Girona**, Spain
**Ter River Park**
1993–1999
DEVELOPER Municipality of Girona
AUTHORS Joaquim Español,
Francesc Hereu
PHOTO Francesc Hereu
**Special Mention 2000**

**London**, United Kingdom
**Opening of Rainham Marshes**
2003–2014
DEVELOPERS Greater London
Authority, London Development
Agency, Design for London,
London Borough of Havering,
Royal Society for the Protection
of Birds / AUTHORS Peter
Beard_LANDROOM, Peter Beard,
Alexander Gore, Sabba Khan,
Dingle Price, Gregory Ross, Mark
Smith, Keita Tajima / PHOTO
Sue Barr
**Special Mention 2014**

**Begues**, Spain
**Vall d'en Joan Landfill Restoration**
2001–2003
DEVELOPERS Barcelona
Metropolitan Area, Municipality of
Barcelona / AUTHORS Enric Batlle,
Joan Roig, Teresa Galí-Izard, Batlle
i Roig Arquitectes / PHOTO Teresa
Galí-Izard
**Joint Winner 2004**

# Waterfront

PHOTO Stipe Surać

**Oslo**, Norway
**Norwegian National Opera**
2000–2008
DEVELOPER Norwegian Government
Agency for Public Construction
and Property Management
AUTHOR Snøhetta
PHOTO Christopher Hagelund
**Joint Winner 2010**

**Marseille**, France
**Vieux Port Renovation**
2011–2013
DEVELOPERS MPM Communauté
urbaine Marseille Provence
Métropole, Direction des
Infrastructures / AUTHORS Michel
Desvigne Paysagiste MDP, Foster +
Partners, Tangram, INGEROP, AIK
PHOTO Michel Desvigne Paysagiste
MDP
**Joint Winner 2014**

**Benidorm**, Spain
**Western Beach Promenade**
2002–2009
DEVELOPERS Government of
Valencia, Municipality of Benidorm

AUTHORS Office of Architecture in Barcelona, Carlos Ferrater, Xavier Martí Galí
PHOTO Alejo Bagué
**Special Mention 2010**

**Copenhagen**, Denmark
**Harbor Bath**
2003
DEVELOPER Municipality of Copenhagen / AUTHORS PLOT (now BIG and JDS) / PHOTO Julien De Smedt
**Special Mention 2004**

**Zadar**, Croatia
**Sea Organ**
2004–2005
DEVELOPERS Port of Zadar, Municipality of Zadar / AUTHOR Nikola Bašic / PHOTO Mladen Radolovic Mrlja
**Joint Winner 2006**

PHOTO Xavier de Cáceres

**Celje**, Slovenia
**New Market**
2006–2010
DEVELOPER Municipality of Celje, CMC Celje
AUTHORS Ark Arhitektura Krušec, Lena Krušec, Tomaž Krušec, Vid Kurinčič

PHOTO Miran Kambič
**Selected 2010**

**Ghent**, Belgium
**Stadshal**
1996–2012
DEVELOPER Municipality of Ghent, TMVW, VVM De Lijn / AUTHORS Robbrecht en Daem architecten, Marie-José van Hee architecten
PHOTO Marc De Blieck, Robbrecht en Daem architecten
**Finalist 2014**

**Figueres**, Spain
**Photovoltaic Cover**
2009–2011
DEVELOPER Municipality of Figueres
AUTHORS Cáceres Arquitectes, Rafael de Cáceres, Xavier de Cáceres / PHOTO Xavier de Cáceres
**Finalist 2012**

**Istanbul**, Turkey
**Beşiktaş Fish Market**
2006–2010
DEVELOPER Municipality of Istanbul Beşiktaş / AUTHOR Gökhan Avcioglu / PHOTO Alp Eren
**Selected 2010**

**Cangas do Morrazo**, Spain
**Fishermen's Huts**
2003–2008
DEVELOPER Harbors of Galicia
AUTHORS Irisarri + Piñera
PHOTO Manuel González Vicente
**Special Mention 2010**

**Ripoll**, Spain
**La Lira Theatre**
2004–2012
DEVELOPER Municipality of Ripoll
AUTHORS RCR Aranda Pigem Vilalta Arquitectes, Joan Puigcorbé
PHOTO David Bravo
**Special Mention 2014**

**Leipzig**, Germany
**Lene Voigt Park**
1998–2002
DEVELOPERS Municipality of Leipzig
AUTHOR Gabriele G. Kiefer, Büro Kiefer / PHOTO Hanns Joosten
**Joint Winner 2002**

PHOTO atelier d'architecture autogérée

**Berlin**, Germany
**Volkspalast**
2002–2005
DEVELOPERS PRISMA Zentrum
fur Standort, Sophiensale HAU
Amelie Deuflhardr / AUTHORS
ZwischenPalast-Nutzung,
Volkspalast Philipp Oswalt
PHOTO David Baltzer
**Special Prize of the Jury 2006**

**Paris**, France
**Passage 56**
2006–2009
DEVELOPER / AUTHOR / PHOTO
atelier d'architecture autogérée
**Special Mention 2010**

**Madrid**, Spain
**Occupation of the Puerta del Sol**
2011
**Special Category 2012**

**Bucharest**, Romania
**Public Swimming Pool**
2012
DEVELOPERS Romanian Order of
Architects, Cartureşti Foundation
AUTHOR / PHOTO studioBasar
**Finalist 2014**

**Arbúcies**, Spain
**SK8+U**
2011–2012
DEVELOPER Skaters, Municipality
of Arbúcies / AUTHORS Straddle3,
Sergi Arenas / PHOTO Straddle3
**Finalist 2014**

**Turin**, Italy
**Barca Workshop**
2011–2013
DEVELOPER / AUTHOR / PHOTO
raumlaborberlin
**Selected 2014**

**Porto**, Portugal
**Fountain Hacks**
2012
DEVELOPER Guimarães European
Capital of Culture 2012

AUTHOR LIKEarchitects, Ricardo
Dourado PHOTO Dinis Sottomayor
**Selected 2014**

**Magdeburg**, Germany
**Open-Air Library**
2005–2009
DEVELOPERS Citizens' Association
of Salbke-Fermersleben-
Westerhüsen, Municipality of
Magdeburg / AUTHORS KARO*,
Architektur+ Netzwerk / PHOTO
Anja Schlamann
**Joint Winner 2010**

**Further information** about the
projects presented in this book
is available at www.publicspace.
org, the web site of the European
Prize for Urban Public Space.

**Other photographic credits**
Cover: David Bravo
p. 158 below: Collectif Etc
p. 159 above: Vladimir Pohtokari
p. 159 below: studioBASAR
p. 160 above: Dinis Sottomayor
p. 160 below: Metaphorm
Architects
p. 164: David Lorente
p. 166, p. 170, p. 178: David Bravo
p. 174: David Lorente

"The City Where I Want to Live",
translated by Clare
Cavanagh from *Without End: New
and Selected Poems* by
Adam Zagajewski.
© 2002 by Adam Zagajewski.
Translation
© 2002 by Farrar, Straus and
Giroux, LLC
Reprinted by permission of Farrar,
Straus and Giroux, LLC and Faber
and Faber Ltd.

**CONSORTIUM OF THE CENTRE DE CULTURA CONTEMPORÀNIA DE BARCELONA**

**PRESIDENT**
Mercè Conesa i Pagès

**VICE PRESIDENT**
Ada Colau Ballano

**GENERAL DIRECTOR**
Vicenç Villatoro Lamolla

The CCCB is a consortium formed by

**EUROPE CITY**

is an initiative of

With support from the Culture Program of the European Union, under the auspices of the "Europe City" project

Based on the
**EUROPEAN PRIZE FOR URBAN PUBLIC SPACE**

is an initiative of
**Centre de Cultura Contemporània de Barcelona**

With the collaboration of
**Architekturzentrum Wien**
**The Architecture Foundation**
**Cité de l'architecture et du patrimoine**
**Deutsches Architekturmuseum**
**Suomen Arkkitehtuurimuseo**
**Muzej za arhitekturo in oblikovanje**

Sponsored by

## EUROPEAN PRIZE FOR URBAN PUBLIC SPACE

**DIRECTOR**
Judit Carrera

**COORDINATION**
Masha Zrnčić

**EDITOR OF WWW.PUBLICSPACE.ORG**
David Bravo

**CONCEPTUALIZATION OF THE WEB PAGE**
Sònia Aran, assessed by David Bravo

## ACKNOWLEDGEMENTS
The Centre de Cultura Contemporània de Barcelona wishes
to thank the following people for their help in producing
this book:

Susana Arias, Magda Anglès, Sergi Masferrer,
Emma Meadows, Lars Müller, Sandra Ollo, Marina Palà,
Guillem Pujadas and Eva Sancho.

Gratitude is also due to all those people who, in recent
years, have given their support to the European Prize
for Urban Public Space and contributed towards the
development of this project:

Patrícia Bas, Gerard Bel, Janina Berzosa, Carlota Broggi,
Teresa Caldeira, Marta Canedo, Neus Carreras,
Mario Corea, Enrique Fibla, Albert Forns, Susana García,
Javier Gascón, Álex Giménez, Marta Giralt, Sara González,
Cristina González, Ilona Hildén, Sara Hoeflich,
Emmi Kattelus, Urša Kosmač Marc, Natalija Lapajne,
Cori Llaveria, Josep Llinàs, Maria Llopis, Jana Manzano,
Cristina Mañas, Àngela Martínez, Olivier Mongin,
Ricard Moya, Carlos Moya, Neus Moyano, Ferran Muñoz,
Mònica Muñoz-Castanyer, Anu Ojala, Lur Olaizola,
Paola Petkova, Elisenda Poch, Nikola Pongrac, Rosa Puig,
Laura Quero, Josep Querol, Josep Ramoneda, Carme Ribas,
Juan Carlos Rodríguez, Gemma Ruiz, Iñaki Sainz,
Núria Salinas, Eva Sitar Jarc, Josep Seuba, Marçal Sintes,
Elías Torres, Zofia Trafas, Maija Valonen, Irene Valverde,
Alexandre Vidal, Julie Wark and Aislinn White.

Special thanks are due to the presidents, secretaries and
all members of the juries for the European Prize for Urban
Public Space.

PRESIDENTS: Oriol Bohigas (2000 and 2004), Josep Llinàs
(2012), Josep Lluís Mateo (2002), Rafael Moneo (2010),
Carme Ribas (2014), Manuel De Solà-Morales (2008) and
Elías Torres (2006).

MEMBERS: Michel Bensa (2000), Aaron Betsky (2002–
2006), Severi Blomsted (2006–2010), Ole Bouman
(2008–2012), Peter Cachola Schmal (2010–2014),
Matevž Čelik (2014), Jan Gehl (2000), Juulia Kauste
(2012–2014), Sarah Mineko Ichioka (2010–2014),
Rowan Moore (2004 and 2008), Lucy Musgrave (2002),
Philippe Paneral (2000), Pierre Pinon (2000),
Francis Rambert (2006–2014), Katharina Ritter (2014),
Manuel de Solà-Morales (2000) and Dietmar Steiner
(2002–2012).

SECRETARIES: David Bravo (2010–2014), Elena Cànovas
(2004), Carles Crosas (2008), Joaquim Español (2002),
Albert Garcia Espuche (2000) and Carme Ribas (2006).

The CCCB also wishes to thank members of the Committee
of Experts who, in recent awards of the Prize, have
nominated specific interventions which have been carried
out in Europe.

Maria Auböck, Ursula Baus, João Belo Rodeia,
Moritz Benoit, Aliaj Besnik, Peter Bishop, Marck Brearly,
Zaš Brezar, Konrad Buhagiar, Viorica Buica, Cosmin
Caciuc, Petra Ceferin, Luigi Centola, François Chaslin,
Daniela Colafranceschi, Marco de Michelis, Pelin Dervis,
Elena Dimitrova, Vladan Djokic, Krzystof Domaradzki,
Marc Dubois, Susanne Dürr, Sándor Finta, Pedro Gadanho,
Sanja Galic-Grozdanic, Sarah Gaventa, Giovanni Ginocchini,
Zaklina Gligorijevic, Kathrin Golda-Pongratz, Nicole
Guichard, Christian Hanak, Gretel Hemgård, Hans Ibelings,
Konstantinos Ioannidis, Mark Isitt, Gabriele Kaiser,
Omer Kanipak, Igor Kovacevic, Ivan Kucina, Christian
Kühn, Esa Laaksonen, Ruta Leitanaite, Michel Lussault,
Josep Lluís Mateo, José Mateus, Mateja Medvedic,
Dan Merta, Vedran Mimica, Ivan Mirkovski, Rusudan
Mirzikashvili, Akos Moravanszky, Henrieta Moravcikova,
Maroje Mrduljas, Krzysztof Nawratek, Tom Nielsen,
Triin Ojari, Osamu Okamura, Richárd Ongjerth, Shane
O'Toole, Darko Polic, Ewa Porebska, Jelena Prokopljevic,
Lena Rahoult, Laszlo Rajk, Sebastian Redecke, Roman
Rutkowski, Jan Schreurs, Bashkim Shehu, Artan Shkreli,
Hjálmar Sveinsson, Fran Tonkiss, Maria Topolcanska,
Vesna Vucinic, Oliver Wainwright, Nathalie Weadick,
Ellis Woodman, Ken Worpole, Ana Maria Zahariade,
Malin Zimm and Karin Åberg Wærn.

We should also like to thank all those people who have
made it possible to present the European Prize for Urban
Public Space exhibition in several European cities.

Diego Albornoz, Karol Barcz, Annette Becker, Lance Jay
Brown, Anaïs Condado, Olga Delidaki, Valerie Disdier,
Myriam Feuchot, Pietro Garau, Laurence Gaussen, Kate
Goodwin, Lucía González, Petra Griefing, Hannu Hellman,
Berit Hoff, Cheryl H. Jacobs, Iyoshi Kreutz, Jacek Lenart,
Elisa Mandiola, Fèlix Manito, Beatriz Marbella,
Jorge Melguizo, Ricardo Mor, Nathalie Montigné,
Manuel Montobbio, Tournikiotis Panayotis, Julien Petit,
Odile Pradel, Klara Pucerova, Isabel Sánchez Jimena,
Annateresa Santangelo, Andrea Seidling, Franco Tagliabue,
Viviana Toledo Orozco, Carlos Uribe and Anouk Wies.

# The Street
## Elías Torres